2021 AMAZON ADS POWER

HOW TO SELL BOOKS BY THE TRUCKLOAD ON AMAZON

Learn how to turn Amazon into your 24/7 sales machine!

PENNY SANSEVIERI

ame
AUTHOR MARKETING EXPERTS

We'd love to hear your feedback!

ame
AUTHOR MARKETING EXPERTS

Author Marketing Experts, Inc.
10601-G Tierrasanta Blvd, Suite 458
San Diego, CA 92124

www.AMarketingExpert.com

© 2021 Penny Sansevieri All rights reserved.
No part of this book may be reproduced in any form or by any electronic or mechanical means, including information storage and retrieval systems, without permission in writing from the publisher, except by a reviewer who may quote brief passages in a review.

Book cover and interior design by
TLC Book Design, TLCBookDesign.com

Truck image: ©Depositphotos.com/uatp12

ISBN: 9798562626929

MORE BOOKS BY PENNY C. SANSEVIERI

NONFICTION

5 Minute Book Marketing for Authors (Amazon Digital 2018, 2019)

52 Ways to Sell More Books (Amazon Digital 2014, 2019)

How to Sell Books by the Truckload on Amazon.com (Amazon Digital 2013, 2018, 2019, 2020)

50 Ways to Sell a Sleigh-Load of Books: Proven Marketing Strategies to Sell More Books for the Holidays (Amazon Digital 2018)

How to Revise and Re-Release Your Book: Simple and Smart Strategies to Sell More Books (Amazon Digital 2018)

Red Hot Internet Publicity – 4th Edition (Amazon Digital 2016)

How to Get a Truckload of Reviews on Amazon.com (Amazon Digital 2013)

Red Hot Internet Publicity (Createspace 2013)

Powerful Pinterest (Amazon Digital 2012)

Get Published Today (Wheatmark, 2012)

52 Ways to Sell More Books (Wheatmark, 2012)

Red Hot Internet Publicity (Cosimo 2010)

Red Hot Internet Publicity (Morgan James Publishing 2007)

From Book to Bestseller (Morgan James Publishing, 2007)

Get Published Today (Morgan James Publishing, 2007)

From Book to Bestseller (PublishingGold.com, Inc., 2005)

No More Rejections: Get Published Today! (Infinity Publishing, 2002, 2003)

Get Published! An Author's Guide to the Online Publishing Revolution (1st Books, 2001)

FICTION

Candlewood Lake (iUniverse, 2005)

The Cliffhanger (iUniverse, 2000)

**To subscribe to our free newsletter,
send an e-mail to subscribe@amarketingexpert.com.**

TABLE OF CONTENTS

HOW TO SELL BOOKS BY THE TRUCKLOAD ON AMAZON.COM..................I

How to Use This Book..3

Understanding Amazon..4

Everything Matters..6

Keyword String Strategies for Greater Visibility........................8

    Understanding Amazon Metadata..9

    Making Your Book More Searchable 9

    Monitoring Keyword Strings 10

    Thinking in Search Engine Terms..11

    The Other Side of Amazon 13

What Publishing Looks Like Now..15

    Short Is the New Long 15

    The Age of the Book Bundle..16

    Combining Forces..16

    The Surge of Audio and Print 17

    The Bar Is Officially Raised..17

    Street Teams and Superfans 18

    Advertising is the New Normal 18

How to Research Keyword Strings 19

    Getting Started..20

    Building Ideas 20

    Searching for Great Keyword Strings on Amazon....................20

    Taking it Step by Step..22

    Finding Keyword Strings with the Highest Searches 23

Quick side note: 24
More Unique Ways to Search 25
Amazon's Search Function 27

Creating Best-Selling Book Ideas 29
Finding Best-Selling Nonfiction Book Ideas 29
Staying on the Short and Narrow 31

Simple Keyword String Success Strategies to Rock your Book 33
Titles and Subtitles 33
Using Descriptive Subtitles 33
Using Keyword Strings from Your Metadata 36
Book Description 37

Understanding Amazon Enhanced Categories 40
Finding the Best Categories on Amazon 41
Changing Your Categories on Amazon 42

Refine: by Themes for Fiction 44

How to Achieve More Visibility for Obscure or Niche Books 46

How Great Amazon Book Descriptions Help Indie Authors Sell More Books 49
Scanning Versus Reading 49
Making Your Description More Scan-Friendly 50
Use Code to Enhance Your Amazon Book Description and Headline 50
Answering "What's in It for Me?" 51
Developing Your Elevator Pitch 53
How Excited Are You? And How Excited Will Your Readers Be? 53
Spell Check 54

Is Your Book Part of a Series? 54
Include Top Keywords 54
Don't Market to Your Ego 55
Include Reviews and Rewards 55
Get a Second Opinion 55
Update Your Page Often 56

How to Write a Kick-Ass Amazon Bio to Sell More Books 58
Start with an Outline and All Book Tie-ins 58
But It's Not Really About You 58
Write in Third Person 59
Show the Reader Your Expertise Without the Ego 59
Add Keyword Strings Particular to Amazon 59
Be Personal (If Appropriate) 60
Be Funny (If Appropriate) 60
Short Is the New Long 61
Include a Call to Action & How Readers Can Find You 61
Customize It & Change It Up 61

Amazon eBook Pricing Tips 62

**How to Boost Your Organic Optimization
with Amazon's Pre-Order 63**
Newly Published 63
Already Published 64
Long Versus Short 64
The Amazon Algorithm for Pre-Orders 65
Promotion 65
Reviews 66
Pricing Your Pre-Order 67
How to Set Up Your Pre-Order 67

The Peril of Amazon's Also-Boughts 69

    Messes with Your Algorithm 70
    May Misrank Your Book(s) 70
    Interrupts the User Experience 71
    Preventing an Also-Bought Mix-Up 71
    Resolving Messed Up Also-Boughts 72

Finding Great Keyword Strings for your Amazon Ads............... 73
    Understanding the Different Keyword Match Types...............74
    Which Match Type is Right for Your Ad Campaign? 75
    Author Names and Book Titles as Keyword Strings 75
    Amazon's Keyword Suggestions..75
    Negative Keyword Strings 76
    Finding Your Keyword Strings 77
    Keyword Strings for Nonfiction..77
    Keyword Strings for Genre Fiction..79
    Keyword Strings for Memoirs,
    Literary Fiction, Women's Fiction 80
    Children's Fiction, Young Adult Fiction 80
    Killing Off Keywords—
    When to Do It and Why You'd Want to....................................80

Product Targeting Ads..82
    Understand Buying Habits 82
    Setting Up Product Targeting Ads...83
    A Final Note on Product Targeting Ads...84

Running Ads Internationally 86

Writing a Great Book Ad.. 87
    Further Customizing Your Ads...87
    Writing Your Ad..88
    Running Ads without Ad Copy...89

Amazon Ads: Reports 90
Amazon Reports 91
FUN AMAZON HACKS 93
Amazon Author Central 94
Farming Data from Amazon Author Central 95
Adding Reviews to Your Book Page via Author Central 95
Follow Author Feature 96
Enhancing Your Amazon Headline 97
Another Boost for Your Books 97
Amazon Video Shorts 99
The Most Overlooked Amazon Sales Tool: International Author Central Pages! 100
Your Author Central Tools 101
Images and Video 101
Your Books 102
The Final Result! 102
How to Access These Pages 102
But Does It Sell Books? 103
Amazon X-Ray 104
Letting Readers Know About X-Ray 106
Making X-Ray Content Fun 106
Creative Ways to Boost Your Keyword Strings 107
10 Smart Ways to Launch Your Book on Amazon 110
Pre-Order 110
Free Book Teaser 111
Book Description 111
Social Proof 112
Book and eBook Pricing 112
Amazon Keyword Strings & Categories 112

    Amazon Ads 113

    Also-Bought 113

    Book Launch, eBook Promos 113

    Spreading Out Your Book Editions 113

Discounted eBook Promotions 114

    Timing Your eBook Promotion 114

    Pricing and Review Strategies 114

    eBook Promotion 115

    Twitter Accounts to Notify 116

    Hashtags to Use 117

    Supporting Your Promotion with Ads 118

How to Combat the Disappearance of Amazon Reviews 119

    Preserve What You've Already Got 119

    Sometimes Amazon has a Glitch 120

    Keep Pushing for Reviews 120

Turning Your Book into a 24/7 Sales Tool 122

    The Benefits of Cross-Promotion 124

    Other Ways You Can Cross-Promote Your Books 124

How to Respond to a Review 126

    How to Respond to Reviews Using Author Central 126

Review Incentives 127

Gifting eBooks 128

Bonus Resources 129

About Penny C. Sansevieri &
Author Marketing Experts, Inc. 132

HOW TO SELL BOOKS BY THE TRUCKLOAD ON AMAZON.COM

HOW TO USE THIS BOOK

As of this writing there are approximately 8 million books on the Amazon site, with more being added every day. According to best estimates, there are 4,500 books published each day in the US, yet only 1% of those authors bother to spend any time optimizing their Amazon page.

What does this mean for you? It means that if you just implement one strategy from this book, you're 90% ahead of most of the authors out there vying for reader attention.

The most efficient way to use this book is to read it from start to finish. But if you're in a rush to acquire some particular knowledge (like the newly updated Amazon Ads section), then feel free to jump ahead. If you're new to the idea of keywords, keyword strings, and enhanced Amazon categories, spend some time in the early chapters getting familiar with terminology and how the Amazon algorithm works.

If you're already an Amazon expert and are just here to brush up on your knowledge, then feel free to skim the chapter headings, which are divided in micro-fashion to allow for easy skimming.

I hope you enjoy this book, and I'd love your thoughts on it, either in a review on Amazon or in a direct email to me: penny@amarketingexpert.com

Wishing you huge Amazon success!

UNDERSTANDING AMAZON

Since I first published this book back in 2017, so much about Amazon has changed that this book not only requires yearly updates—it demands it. Now, in 2020—almost 2021—things are trickier than ever. As you'll see in the next chapter, when it comes to Amazon, now more than ever, *everything* you do matters. This is why the content of this book has become so crucial.

It's not an understatement to say that Amazon has changed everything about book publishing and promotion. It seems like every time Amazon introduces something, the competition jumps on the bandwagon, and creates similar products or experiences on their sites.

This is a problem, because the Amazon ecosystem is a tremendous game-changer. Much like Google, it can not only help you find exactly the right book you've been looking for, but it can also show you things you never knew you needed.

That's the power of the algorithm, and it's also the power of the ads.

I've talked about how alike Amazon and Google are which makes sense when you consider that Bezos was an early investor in Google and had the inside track learning how Google worked as it developed into the behemoth Google is today. Actually, the algorithms of Google and Amazon are quite similar.

But to dissect and understand Amazon is like taking Google apart piece by piece. No one person can do that, but we can uncover various algorithms that can help you achieve more visibility for your book.

However, this book is not a quick fix. Why? Because when it comes to Amazon, there are no quick fixes. There's no one single solution. But there are several strategies that, when implemented in tandem, help create the most optimal visibility for your book.

While many experts talk about keyword strings, categories and pricing, few experts mention this important fact:

Amazon is more of a search engine than it is a store. In fact, Amazon is literally the "Google" of online buying.

And with this model in mind, I need to tell you right up front that there is no instant anything when it comes to ranking on Amazon. There's a lot of shortcut software out there, and keyword apps, but time and time again, I've been reminded that there's nothing like good old-fashioned hard work to make your Amazon page soar. Much like ranking on Google, people are always searching for shortcuts, but they rarely work.

Understanding Amazon and knowing how to use it to your advantage are vital to keeping those sales up. Amazon is *the* place for book marketing today. All the way back to June of 2014, *SEOMoz*, a popular search engine optimization blog, talked about Amazon and its ranking system. It said, "If you're an author, you don't care about ranking on Google. You want to rank on Amazon."

Everyone in the search engine world knows Amazon ceased being "just a store" several years ago. Now they are the go-to for anything from books and electronics to fashion and pet food.

And here's another twist: Amazon just launched their Explore website, which is a site designed to create virtual experiences for travelers. Pretty smart, considering the pandemic, yes? Previously Amazon dug into the travel market, and now they're exploring car sales.

The problem is, all of this digs right at the heart of Google's business. Think about it. With Amazon Explore you can get access to destinations, with their grocery service you can buy food and other sundry items, with their vehicle service, you can buy a car. This kind of market domination means sites like Yelp and Google's own review systems will start playing second fiddle to Amazon's long-standing and quite extensive review system. And as these Amazon portals become successful, you could go to this one-stop-shop to find everything from a trip to Maui (virtual or in person) to a contractor for your room addition.

And let's not forget Amazon Music, Amazon grocery stores, and their Echo technology. Think I'm crazy? Ten years ago, no one thought Amazon would sell anything besides books. This company is making serious moves.

Essentially, it means that Amazon is gearing up to play a whole different game, a game that means more and more people will be searching on Amazon for practically everything they need.

And if it isn't already, Google should be worried.

EVERYTHING MATTERS

When I teach authors about websites and optimizing them for maximum visibility on Google, I remind students that absolutely everything matters to Google. In order to get great search rank, leave no stone unturned. Every page, every keyword, every image is counted for or against you in terms of ranking.

The same is true with Amazon.

And when I say that everything matters when it comes to ranking on Amazon I mean: everything.

Remember that first book you published that didn't do well? The cover wasn't great, you knew it could have or should have been better—but it was your first book, so you took in in stride. You learned from your mistakes and you moved on.

The thing is, Amazon never moves on. Somewhere, lurking in the backend of Amazon is a black mark beside your name, and that mark reads: *this author once published a book no one seemed to like = low relevancy.*

Amazon cares about relevancy, it's how their entire site—with all of its millions of products, manages to find exactly the right thing you're looking for, when you need it. Plug in a few keywords and boom, the exact widget, lotion or book you were looking for appears. This is why relevancy is so important, and why making sure everything that's connected to your Amazon account (even the older books you've published) is in tiptop shape. This point can't be overemphasized.

The same is true for Amazon ads. If you're running ads for a book that's getting very few engagements (Click-through rate), Amazon's internal search engine will give you a checkmark by "low relevancy." We'll dig into more of this as we explore the Amazon ads chapter—and every chapter from that point forward. There's also a rumor that if your ads never seem to do well across the board, Amazon will ding your relevancy score as well. If you have an ad set that's not doing well, kill it. We'll dig into more of this later in the ads section.

What if you have an older book that's not doing so great? Do you leave it and hope for the best, or republish it and breathe new life into an old book? We'll explore that as well.

For now, just remember that each piece of the Amazon puzzle impacts the other pieces, and everything you do impacts everything else. It all matters. The good news? It's easier than ever to get back on track, and small changes and enhancements can help build your status within the Amazon ecosystem and grow your presence for both your author page, and your book pages.

KEYWORD STRING STRATEGIES FOR GREATER VISIBILITY

Returning to the similarity between Amazon's algorithm and Google's algorithm, when you want a website to rank on Google, you need a well-chosen set of keyword strings on the homepage, ideally in the copy. It's also smart to have keyword strings in your website address to boost your search visibility.

Though Amazon responds differently, the idea is still the same.

First, let's take a look at the six keys to Amazon ranking:

- Popularity of your title
- Matching search term
- Social proof/reviews
- Pricing strategy
- Book page
- Amazon ads

We'll cover each of these in this book.

Despite the insane number of books on Amazon, you can still be on page one or claim the number one ranking.

Why? Because most people aren't aware that Amazon is its own search engine. But now you are aware, and you can use the information to your advantage. Keep in mind that the tools shared in this book won't guarantee your book hits the number one spot on Amazon, but they will help you generate a significant amount of attention. In the end, isn't that what you want?

UNDERSTANDING AMAZON METADATA

There was a time when no one talked about metadata. Now it's a buzzword. But metadata means different things, depending on the website where you're planning to sell your book. Amazon differs from other sites, and it's important to know why:

The only things related to metadata that Amazon cares about are your keyword strings and your book's (enhanced) categories.

Zeroing in on Amazon's metadata is a fantastic way to generate more attention for your book, and the great thing is, everything counts. Your book title, subtitle, and keyword strings, literally everything matters, and I'll break this down throughout this book.

But first let's take a closer look at metadata, so you can see what I mean.

MAKING YOUR BOOK MORE SEARCHABLE

The more searchable your book is, the more often it's going to come up in searches, and consequently, the more you'll sell.

Part of this is due to Amazon's metadata, which is available to every author who has their book on Amazon, but most authors and publishers don't use it or understand it. It's not because they're lazy, but because it's complex and ever-changing.

KDP, Amazon's Kindle Direct Publishing program and Amazon's eBook arm, is a popular way to get your book onto the Amazon platform. But it isn't the only way to populate keyword strings into the Amazon system. If you've published through another service that allows you to populate keywords into your metadata, these will wind up helping you on the Amazon site as well, because those keywords will get pushed through that system as well as any you set up directly on the KDP dashboard.

For the purposes of this chapter, and to keep it simple, I'm going to focus on the KDP dashboard. Just know that everything you learn here can be applied to virtually any dashboard you publish on.

If you're reading this and you're traditionally published, this information will work, too. Later in this book I'll show you how to do this search and hand the results over to your publisher.

If you've published on Amazon via KDP, the screenshot of the dashboard below will probably look familiar to you. This dashboard is where you access all of your books' metadata—except the enhanced categories, which I'll discuss in a bit.

Keywords — Enter up to 7 search keywords that describe your book.
Your Keywords (Optional)
- Book marketing
- How to market a book
- Book marketing for authors
- Amazon marketing
- Book promotion
- Amazon marketing services
- Sell more books

Categories — Choose up to two browse categories.
- Nonfiction > Language Arts & Disciplines > Authorship
- Nonfiction > Business & Economics > Marketing > General

You can see you're allowed up to seven search keywords, which should be keyword phrases, or strings.

Although Amazon says they're optional, they should *never* be optional, nor overlooked. While I was doing research for this book, I asked ten authors to let me take a look at the back end, behind-the-scenes details of their books, with the caveat that I wouldn't add terms they didn't need. *None* of them had search words listed. Categories are always a given—all my authors had chosen their categories—but search keywords (and enhanced categories) are too often ignored.

We're going to dig into keyword string strategies in a few chapters, but for now just start percolating some ideas. No doubt, you've also seen from the above screenshot that I'm using keyword strings and *not* single keywords. In a minute, I'll discuss why.

MONITORING KEYWORD STRINGS

Once you've selected your keyword strings, it's important to monitor them regularly. And you may not want to stick with the same strings for the duration of your book's life on Amazon.

Why? Because search habits change. some searches are more popular than others, and you won't know which will get you the most bounce until you start experimenting with a variety of terms. I recommend you start a spreadsheet with the various keyword strings you've selected for your book and keep track of your book's ranking whenever you search these terms.

> Do not, under any circumstances, use anything other than standard words and phrases for your keyword strings. You can use words and phrases like "romance," "contemporary romance," and even things like, "Kindle deals under $3.99," as long as your book fits that pricing.
>
> But you can no longer use author names and/or book titles. However, as we'll discuss later in this book, you can use names and/or titles with the Amazon Ad System. But for metadata-related keyword strings, it's still against Amazon's Terms of Service.

THINKING IN SEARCH ENGINE TERMS

As you'll learn throughout this book, work you do on Amazon is similar to what I would recommend if you were trying to get traction on Google for your website. This is the mindset you must embrace. Unfortunately, I haven't found discussions of this mindset in many of the books I've read on this topic.

Therein lies yet another problem:

When the first edition of this book came out, there were dozens of "How to Sell on Amazon" books on the market. Now the number has dwindled to just a few.

Why? I think a lot of it has to do with the fact that Amazon is tough to monitor. The algorithm changes a lot, and it's essential to keep an eye on this if you want your book to be successful. Also, it's a lot to keep track of. If you want to stay current with what Amazon is doing, then once you've finished reading this book, consider signing up for our Master Amazon Video Program available here: www.amarketingexpert.com/master-amazon-video-series.

So, back to our search engine mindset.
Using this methodology, it becomes clear that in order to get ranking for your website, you need a few things:

1. **Metadata:** Keyword strings that your market is searching for.

2. **An attractive website:** Believe me, the days of Google ranking bad-looking sites are over. Today you need, a solid, attractive website. I don't mean pretty, just no sloppy train wrecks cobbled together without a purpose or user-friendly navigation.

3. **Consistent blog posts:** Google likes this, because it tells Google the site is being updated frequently, which helps your search results.

Now, if we turn to Amazon, and translate this to book/product speak, we see that similar rules apply:

1. **Metadata:** Keywords, keywords, keywords—Amazon loves keywords (i.e. keyword strings) and applying that knowledge skillfully will help you achieve better ranking.

2. **A good book cover:** While Amazon may not ding you for a bad-looking cover, your potential readers most certainly will.

3. **Reviews:** Consistently getting new reviews is likened to blogging on your website on a regular basis. It shows there's consistent activity. Reviews also help with the visibility of your page and your ranking on Amazon—even if your book is a few years old.

4. **Amazon Ads:** I've mentioned this before, relative to Amazon ads, and we'll dig into this more in the ads chapter.

5. **Book Page:** Much like your website, your Amazon book page should be peppered with keywords.

I'll go into each of these in more depth later on in the book!

THE OTHER SIDE OF AMAZON

In addition to the search engine side of Amazon, there is still the store, and, as a retailer, Amazon's goal is to sell stuff, and a lot of it.

We'll talk in more depth about the retailer aspect later on in this book, but the one thing I've learned is that most authors list their books on Amazon and think they're done. They just assume Amazon will do the selling for them. This couldn't be further from the truth. There are certain strategies you must implement before you can relax a bit.

Aside from being a great place to sell your book, Amazon can become an author's best friend with the application of a little bit of know-how.

In addition to the mysterious search engine component I will unravel for you shortly, there's also the brick-and-mortar type sales model Amazon uses. This model is essentially a big piece of their algorithm.

Let's say you're the manager of a clothing store, and one day you notice your cashmere sweaters (last season's style) are selling. Normally you wouldn't put them at the front of your store, since you leave that area for the "known hits"—meaning the most trending products, the ones you know will sell well, right? But when something you hadn't expected to sell at all starts gaining interest, you naturally figure it's a good idea to give it more exposure—you put it a bit closer to the front.

Now the sweaters are selling even faster and you move them to one of the front tables. Bingo! You sell even more. Then one day, when you're redoing your storefront window, you think: *Let's display them here.* Suddenly your stock is sold out.

This is essentially what happens with Amazon, except replace the sweater with your book. When your book starts selling on Amazon, this superstore takes notice, and your book starts popping up in all sorts of places that relate to book recommendations.

If you own a Kindle, you know when you're looking to buy a book or have just finished reading one, the system shows you other books on the same or similar topics? This is one of the many ways Amazon pushes a book that's selling or showing great promise.

Have you ever wished you could see your book there?

How, exactly, does it happen, and how can you make it work for you?

That's where the algorithm/search engine model and this book come into play. What I'll show you relates to algorithm triggers within Amazon's search function.

Almost 100% of the time, when I look at Amazon author profiles, I find that authors aren't doing much to promote their titles. Many of your book promotion tasks require your own "marketing muscle." Much of that marketing muscle is actually marketing know-how—a skill most of us aren't born with.

Regardless of the age of your book, if your subject matter is still relevant, you can boost it on Amazon using these techniques. I've seen it happen with books that are five years old or more. If you're reading this and wondering if you can make it work for your book, let me assure you, you can!

With the exception of Amazon ads, everything I recommend in this book is free and will only cost you the time spent on research and tracking. As I mentioned earlier, some things I show you may have immediate results, others will take a bit of time.

Once you implement these strategies, however, it's a bit of "set it and forget it," meaning that once you've done the heavy lifting, the algorithm kicks in and Amazon does the rest.

WHAT PUBLISHING LOOKS LIKE NOW

As I mentioned earlier, 4,500 books are published *every day* in the United States, and while that number is staggering, it's not even close to being accurate.

Why? Because it only includes ISBNs registered in the system. It doesn't count books uploaded straight to Amazon using their internal ASIN number.

Think about this for a minute. How does the staggering number of books published daily affect your title?

Well, for one thing, it makes your book harder to find. Therefore, putting intelligent, informed effort into your Amazon page is crucial. But also consider whether having only one book out there is enough to draw attention to yourself and your brand.

In this chapter, we'll look at a few other success strategies you may want to incorporate in your marketing plan.

SHORT IS THE NEW LONG

In most cases, having one book isn't enough to gain traction, because often your first book is your loss leader. It's hard to hear, but it's true—at least in most cases. And while your book may be the exception, I've learned having multiple books out there is a smart idea.

If you find the thought of publishing multiple books discouraging, consider this: The books don't have to be long. This book, for example is actually two books. Each is between 70 and 80 pages each. Not all that long, right?

Short is the new long. I've spoken to a number of fiction authors who've said their 50- to 75-page novellas are doing better than their longer counterparts. Shorter books are selling. Which means you could release one long book a year and then boost sales by publishing a few novellas or shorter nonfiction how-to guides, manuals, and so on. As long as they're relevant, helpful, and/or entertaining, there's no reason they can't continue to sell, which will help enhance your bookshelf presence on Amazon.

THE AGE OF THE BOOK BUNDLE

Bundling isn't new, but it is hot, and it's not just for fiction. I've done book bundles for my nonfiction books, too. Remember, long books are not going away, but these days shorter books are having a significant impact on sales. Book bundles are another great way to own the "virtual shelf," or search results page, which also helps with your Amazon visibility.

Consider this: If you have both short and longer books, or a longer book you've serialized by chopping it up into two, three, or four parts—and someone goes searching on Amazon for your topic, wouldn't it be nice to fill the Amazon search page with your book? That's an additional benefit of the book bundle.

I was at a writers' conference recently where an author asked me what he could do with his older, 400-page sci-fi novel. He wanted to re-release it. I suggested he divide the book into four parts, releasing each as a separate book on Amazon, and then bundle them into the full novel.

If you take this route, however, with a series that's tightly connected (meaning a continuation), make sure you have a page at the beginning of each book summarizing the previous book, and at the back of each book to lead the reader to the next book in the series.

Splitting up your books and bundling them will also revive your publication date and bring it current.

It will open up options for promotion and reviews, too.

COMBINING FORCES

I've also noticed authors collaborating on book bundles. In fact, even big-name, best-selling authors are doing it. With the rising popularity of the book bundle, I think we'll see a lot more of them.

I've talked with a few authors who are combining their titles with other authors' titles just so they can keep putting out fresh titles on Amazon. With all the new books out there, it's going to be important for authors with a strong following to support each other by combining books, and perhaps even combining book tours.

In addition to novellas and book bundles, including different authors combining their efforts, I'm seeing more audio books on the market. Offering your books in a variety of formats will be important going forward.

THE SURGE OF AUDIO AND PRINT

While eBooks will continue to be popular, authors who have gone exclusively to eBooks are learning it's important to make their books available in multiple formats in order to stay competitive.

It's never a bad idea to have a book in print. In fact, if you want to succeed in spite of the deluge of new titles published every year, it's wise to have your book in eBook format, print *and* in audio format. Audiobook popularity is growing rapidly, with new titles emerging from this channel all the time, including a lot of indie titles previously available in eBook format only. As indie publishing continues to grow, books available in multiple formats will stand out from those in eBook format only.

We'll address the benefits of print later.

THE BAR IS OFFICIALLY RAISED

It's here—that raised bar we all keep talking about. With the hundreds and thousands of books now published, many (more than ever) will go unnoticed. *Right now the average sale for a self-published book is one hundred copies. Total. Forever.*

I predict that number will drop to ten or less. Shocking? Not really. Fewer than 1% of all books published will ever make it to bookstore shelves. A lot of authors aren't prepared for the marketing or the work it takes to get their book out there, and keep it there. Now more than ever, you'll need not just a good product, but an outstanding one.

One of the reviewers we work with says the biggest reason she turns down a book is because it lacks good editing. Many indie titles suffer from this, unfortunately. The days of shortcuts, self-editing, and self-designed covers are gone. Bring your A-game, or don't play at all.

STREET TEAMS AND SUPERFANS

Now, more than ever before, it's important to engage your fans. A few writing events I spoke at talked about "street teams," but "superfans" is essentially the same concept: Get fans to help you sell books. I mention both here, so you'll recognize the terminology when you see and hear it.

Okay, how do you make this strategy work for you? I plan to publish From Book to Bestseller in the near future, which will have a dedicated chapter on Superfans but here is some help to get you started.

You need to make your readership feel important. Make them feel as though they're a critical element in the success of the book, because they are! Offer them exclusive specials and incentives. Remind them often how important they are to you and offer them free "swag" (fun promotional gifts like coffee mugs or bookmarks) to share with their friends (other potential readers).

One of the authors at a Romance Writers of America conference talked about a reader who owns a hair salon. This author sent sample books, bookmarks, and other swag for her friend to put in the shop. It went over so well the salon owner keeps asking for more.

Be creative with your street teams, and if you need help with something, ask them. You'll be surprised how quickly reader/author bonds are formed, and how readers who love your books are willing to go the extra mile.

ADVERTISING IS THE NEW NORMAL

Advertising on sites like Amazon, on social media, and through book-specific platforms like BookBub, is quickly becoming a staple for successful authors, who realize it's getting harder and harder to stay in front of potential buyers and new fans in between releases. It's also a relatively self-sustaining strategy once you become adept at analyzing your ad's performance and modifying as you go.

HOW TO RESEARCH KEYWORD STRINGS

When you built your website, your web designer most likely asked you about keywords. Most of you had no idea what keywords were unless you had someone helping you, and odds are you gave your designer a blank stare. Maybe you offered them a few keywords you thought might help, but in all likelihood the ones you came up with weren't very helpful.

When we talk about keywords, it's very important to think in terms of keyword *strings*, because that's how people search. Consider the last search you did on Google. Did you pop in one keyword like *mystery* or *romance*? Likely not. You probably plugged in a string of keywords like, "most romantic weekend getaways," or, "best mystery dinner theatres." Whether you're talking about Google or Amazon searches, they both respond better to keyword strings than to single keywords.

Just about everything we'll talk about ties back to your keyword strings, which is why I decided to include this in-depth discussion that unpacks the often-mysterious concept. You'll likely refer to this chapter often, since various places in the book will tie back to it.

Finally, the keyword strings we're looking at will all fall under a basic economic principle: supply and demand. Meaning that what we're aiming for is very little supply for something that's in high demand.

This chapter will show you exactly how to do that.

AMAZON TIP!

You're allowed up to seven keyword strings when you upload your book to Amazon's KDP. I suggest you come up with a minimum of fifteen keyword strings while you're doing research, so you can swap them out and/or use them in your book description, product page blurbs, enhanced book description, review pitches, and so on.

GETTING STARTED

When you're starting out, finding keyword strings can seem like an arduous and complex task, but it doesn't have to be. I'll show you a few simple ways to build your keyword strings on Amazon. I'd start by carving out an hour or so to start building your list.

What About Using Software?

Generally, I'm opposed to keyword software because I always find that the searches on Amazon tend to be more accurate. However, I have used the *Google Adword Planner*, as I'll discuss in a bit, as well as *Keywords Everywhere*, which I'll share with you as well.

The best kinds of keyword strings are ones you find manually. Why? Because with so many books being published on Amazon, it would be hard for any software—even Google's robust *Keyword Planner*—to give you 100% accurate results. Seeing it with your own eyes is the only way to truly validate your choices.

BUILDING IDEAS

It always helps if you know the keywords and keyword strings your audience tends to use. If you don't know—and this often happens with nonfiction authors, you'll want to start by testing some keyword strings to find out what seems to work well for your book, subject matter, niche, or genre.

SEARCHING FOR GREAT KEYWORD STRINGS ON AMAZON

If you're doing a search on Amazon to find keyword strings for your Kindle Direct Publishing dashboard and individual books, I suggest by starting on the Kindle side of the Amazon website.

Not every search is created equal; searching for "mystery and suspense" on the main Amazon site instead of digging down into the Kindle department specifically, will net you very different and largely inaccurate results.

Since so many books are eBooks only, that side of Amazon is denser than their print book side and yields a better representation of what you're really competing against.

To begin your keyword string search, first select Kindle Store from the dropdown (left-hand side of the search below), leaving the search bar blank, and click the orange search button (with the magnifying glass symbol).

Next, click "Kindle eBooks."

Once you're there, just start typing your keywords into the search bar. While you're keying them in, Amazon's intuitive search will start to drop down suggestions. Not all of the suggestions will be ones you'll use, but they're certainly a good start.

Ideally you want your keyword string to match the following criteria:

- Make sure you're only using keyword *strings*. Do not settle for single keywords, because consumers don't search that way. You wouldn't Google with just the word "suspense," either.

- Don't assume Amazon's recommendations, such as those from the above screenshot, are the exact right ones for your book. We'll look at how to determine that in a minute.

- Once you've collected Amazon's suggestions, you'll want to pop over to those pages and see what kinds of books are listed on the results page, AND what their sales rank is. Because if you're using a keyword string with a very high sales rank, it means not many people are actually using that particular keyword string. We'll discuss this later in the book.

- Be sure to notice whether there are a number of free books cluttering the first page of a particular keyword string search. Let's say you're looking at "suspense mystery books."
You may notice lots of books on free promotion, which will always be at the top of the list. Don't bother to look at their sales rank, because it's not an accurate depiction of how this string is actually doing. Instead, keep going down the list until you find a book that isn't on a pricing promo.

- Don't worry if the search string includes books in Kindle Unlimited. It won't affect your results.

TAKING IT STEP BY STEP

Let's break this down even further. Say you have a book that teaches you how to create a home office, or build a business from home, and so on. The keyword string I'd start with would be: *working from home*. You'll notice from the screenshot below that the number of books in that particular search term is only 2,000, meaning a relatively low supply. Considering that there are 7 million books on Amazon (and growing daily), 2,000 books is a reasonably low number. In terms of "supply" we're in a good place. Next up we're going to check the demand for this keyword string.

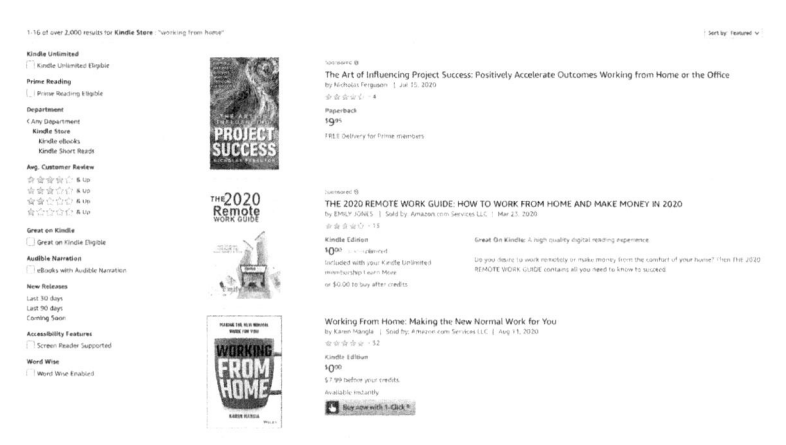

It's important to note here that the search that's popped up is a list of books that are somewhat older, which does not impact the integrity of the keyword string. Next, I'm going to click on the first three books to check their sales ranks. Note: none of the books at the top of this string were new, but their sales ranks were all pretty impressive.

As I clicked through these books, I discovered that age wasn't a factor in their success—they all seemed to be doing well. Sales rankings were low, which was a solid indicator and means we now have a keyword string that exactly meets the right criteria: low supply, high demand. You'll want to do this several more times until you have all the keyword strings you'll need.

Sales rank indicates a book's sales in relation to other books' sales. A book ranked number 1 has sold the most. So, a large number on the sales rank line isn't good. A book ranking of 88,453 means that 88,452 books are selling better than it is. A great high-sales rank is normally 10,000 or less.

But this ranking also depends to some degree on the genre, niche, or subject matter. For example, a sales rank of 13,000 may not seem great. But for some of my own nonfiction stuff it means they're selling pretty well. In some cases, I'm doing $500-plus in book sales per month at that sales rank. However, when I look at that 13,000 rank in fiction, the sales are often lower.

Anything you've heard about how sales rank works should be taken with a grain of salt, because the numbers can vary depending on the category (genre, niche, or subject matter).

Now let's dig into another example. Let's say you have a royal romance book, so you go onto Amazon and type in "royal romance." The keyword string shows a relatively low number of books considering the popularity of the genre—as of this writing I'm showing around 6,000 (you might want to verify this along with me, it's good practice)!

While 6,000 may seem high to you, consider how busy the genre is. Romance of any kind is a heavily populated category, so I went with this keyword string and checked the sales rank of the titles. I was pleasantly surprised by what I found, meaning each of the books under that particular search string had a fairly low sales rank.

FINDING KEYWORD STRINGS WITH THE HIGHEST SEARCHES

As you start searching for keywords, it's important to know that beyond being a popular search term on Amazon, the ideal keyword string also leads you to books that are selling well, and this is called a "funnel." Surprisingly, not all keyword strings, even those that rank high on Amazon, are terrific funnels. Why? Because although they may be searched frequently, they might not have the types of books your consumer wants. In other words, for whatever reason, consumers aren't buying the books that show up on these searches.

Often this happens when books are populated to a particular category that doesn't have heavy traffic. The suggestions that pop up on Amazon are suggestions based on frequent *searches*, not sales. Suggested search strings don't necessarily mean they have a high enough frequency of search or enough buyers looking at that category to boost your book sales. It simply means that the string is being searched often enough to be noticed and included by an algorithm.

The general rule about supply and demand comes with a few exceptions. You may find a keyword string with a small number of books in it, but checking the sales rank makes you second-guess your options, because the sales rank number is very large (meaning the book in question isn't selling a lot of copies). This can happen with some keyword strings. Some may have a small number of books, but the sales rank number on the books is pretty high, generally in the one hundred thousands. This means that, yes, there are a small number of books under that search term. But it also means they aren't selling.

The flip side of this is when you think, "Okay, I'll put my book in there and get to the number one spot with little or no effort."

I thought that too, and I shifted a romance book into a narrow keyword string. The book fell like a rock in the rankings, which points us back to this important thing to keep in mind: even if Amazon suggests the keyword string, you still need to do your own homework to make sure it's the right choice for you.

QUICK SIDE NOTE:

On another example search of "romance and military," I found that the first few titles did not have a great sales ranking, but **then** the covers weren't stellar either. I'm betting that the books ranked lower because they tinkered with the keywords in the subtitle, which would help these books for a time, but ultimately **they would** drop off the search **due** to low sales.

As I dug down this list, I found other books that did have a high sales rank. So don't be tricked by the first few books. If their sales ranks are bad, but it's an ideal keyword string for your book, go deeper. Click down to other titles on page one and see if their sales ranks are better. Very often they will be.

MORE UNIQUE WAYS TO SEARCH

If you've tried to find something on Google, you have most likely used a search string that involves the word, "and." For example, you entered, "Mystery and book," or something along those lines. The same type of search string works on Amazon, but there's a bit of a twist to it. Let me show you what I mean.

Let's say you wrote a romance novel, and you're trying to find out what your potential readers are searching for. Head on over to Amazon and type in, "Romance and," and see what pops up:

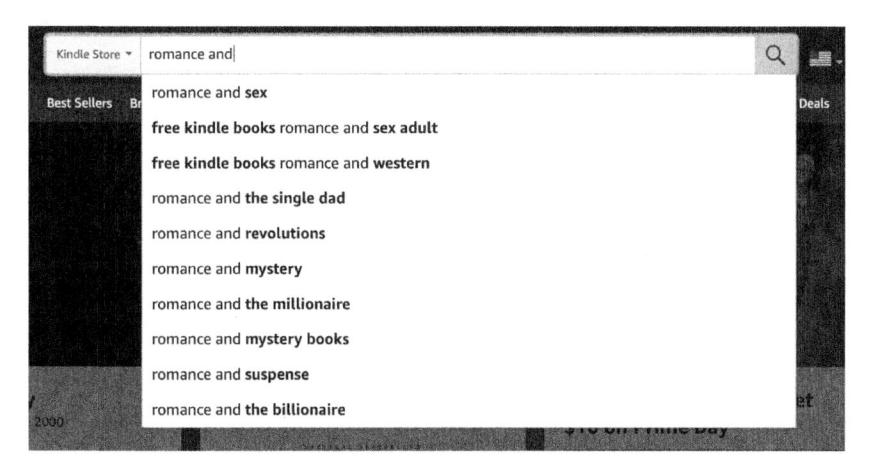

```
Kindle Store ▼   romance and                                                Q
Best Sellers  Br   romance and sex                                               Deals
                   free kindle books romance and sex adult
                   free kindle books romance and western
                   romance and the single dad
                   romance and revolutions
                   romance and mystery
                   romance and the millionaire
                   romance and mystery books
                   romance and suspense
                   romance and the billionaire
```

These are autosuggestions based on your keyword plus the word, "and." Now let's take this a step further. Let's add the beginnings of another letter to this, creating a search string that looks like this: "Romance and s." Take a look at the screenshot on the following page:

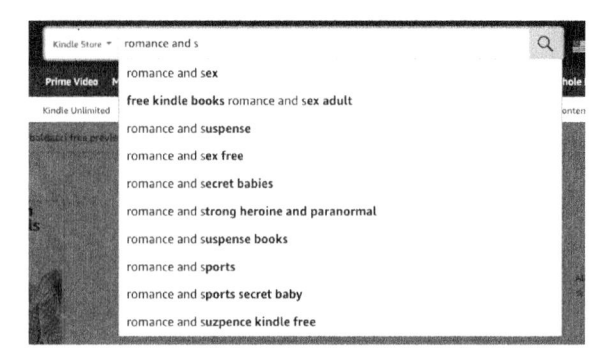

```
Kindle Store ▼    romance and s
                  romance and sex
                  free kindle books romance and sex adult
                  romance and suspense
                  romance and sex free
                  romance and secret babies
                  romance and strong heroine and paranormal
                  romance and suspense books
                  romance and sports
                  romance and sports secret baby
                  romance and suzpence kindle free
```

You can see that it brings up even more search suggestions—and possible ideas for more keywords.

Although it doesn't typically happen in fiction as much as it does in nonfiction, it's still a good idea to remember there are certain keyword strings that change seasonally. Seasonal tie-ins to your topic should be factored into the keyword string *only as long as that string is getting enough searches*, which we'll cover in the next chapter.

With non-fiction you can see changes in searches with what's going on in the news or major shifts in industry trends. So as long as you're an expert on your topic and keeping up with what's going on in your industry you could really benefit from doing some keyword research to see if searches on Amazon have shifted in a way you can take advantage of as well.

Now you know a little more about the different ways to search for optimal keyword strings. Depending on your subject, genre, or niche, you may want to try them all. But remember, if you decide to change your keyword strings, be sure to add them to your book description, and maybe even incorporate them in your title if your book's not "on the shelves" yet.

Also be sure people are actually buying the books in the search results using the keyword strings you're considering. Check the sales rank to be sure it's not too large/high.

Now you've learned the tools for searching keyword strings and how to use them. You can make use of your knowledge on many levels while you get ready to publish a book that will sell, or market a book that isn't selling well…yet.

AMAZON'S SEARCH FUNCTION

As we discussed in this chapter, Amazon's search function will drop down suggestions in much the same way that Google's does. But there's a right way and a wrong way to use it.

Take a look at the screenshot below. I typed in, "selling books," and Amazon's top suggestions for this particular keyword string are:

```
Kindle Store ▼   selling books
Best Sellers    best selling books
                    in All Departments
                    in Amazon Warehouse
                best selling books 2020 fiction
                selling books on amazon for cash
                selling books on amazon
                selling books
```

This is where things start to get interesting, because these search suggestions from Amazon will show you what's trending with their consumers. If you click on one of the search terms, like, "selling books on Amazon," it will take you to the page below, where you'll see another technique for increasing visibility: Several of these authors (including yours truly) have included the popular search term in their title, which also helps with their ranking. We'll discuss this more later, too.

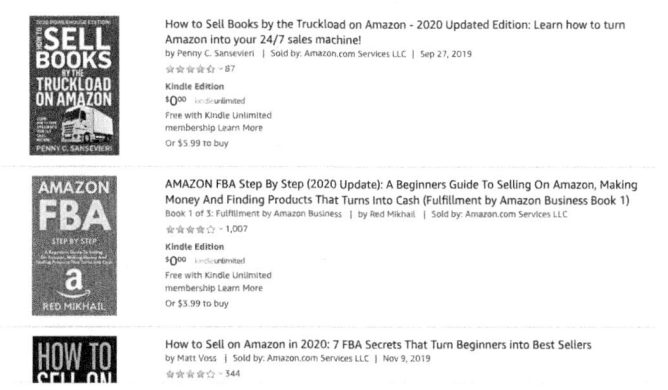

How to Sell Books by the Truckload on Amazon - 2020 Updated Edition: Learn how to turn Amazon into your 24/7 sales machine!
by Penny C. Sansevieri | Sold by: Amazon.com Services LLC | Sep 27, 2019
★★★★☆ · 87
Kindle Edition
$0.00 kindleunlimited
Free with Kindle Unlimited membership Learn More
Or $5.99 to buy

AMAZON FBA Step By Step (2020 Update): A Beginners Guide To Selling On Amazon, Making Money And Finding Products That Turns Into Cash (Fulfillment by Amazon Business Book 1)
Book 1 of 1: Fulfillment by Amazon Business | by Red Mikhail | Sold by: Amazon.com Services LLC
★★★★☆ · 1,007
Kindle Edition
$0.00 kindleunlimited
Free with Kindle Unlimited membership Learn More
Or $3.99 to buy

How to Sell on Amazon in 2020: 7 FBA Secrets That Turn Beginners into Best Sellers
by Matt Voss | Sold by: Amazon.com Services LLC | Nov 9, 2019
★★★★☆ · 344

If you've already published your book (and likely most of you reading this are in this category), don't worry. There are a lot of other things you can do to help spike your book sales that don't involve changing the title, at least on the cover. Subtitles with keyword strings *can* be added to product pages, though.

If you haven't put a name on your book yet, you may want to seriously consider using this method to find and use some hot, trending Amazon keywords or keyword strings to include in your title!

CREATING BEST-SELLING BOOK IDEAS

It's one thing to write a book. It's quite another to write a book that will sell. We all want to follow our passion, write our dream, and dance creatively with our muse.

But wouldn't it be fantastic if, amidst all this creativity, we also manage to produce a best-selling book? That is, after all, part of the dream. This chapter discusses several things you can do to ensure your book targets the largest audience possible.

FINDING BEST-SELLING NONFICTION BOOK IDEAS

I know a gal who's keyed in to a bunch of SEO people. For those of you not familiar with the term, SEO stands for Search Engine Optimization. These are the folks who spend their lives trying to get on the first page of Google.

Several years back we were talking about how to create ideas that sell. She told me many of her SEO buddies literally write books based only on keywords and keyword strings. It has nothing to do with their passion or even what they want to write about. They focus on "saleable terms," meaning phrases getting a huge bounce on Google. This may not be how you'd normally think about writing a book, but there are merits to this methodology. Here are a few things to think about while you plan what to write about:

Book focus: Where will you focus your book? What subject or theme do you want to write about? Don't get too caught up in a set plan. Leave some room for flexibility, but do consider what's hot right now. Your original idea may have been the starting point, but, depending on how long you've been sitting on it, there's a solid chance you can update it a bit to ensure you're responding to current market needs, or to make yourself stand out from competitive titles that hit the market before you.

- **Book title:** As I mentioned before, a book title is a great place to use keyword strings, so keep an open mind about reworking your title as it gets closer to your publication date. This is also the perfect time for some market research, because besides the need for hot, keyword strings, a title should also answer a question or the pique the interest of your potential buyers. Often you're too close to your own work to be aware of hot, trending possibilities…unless you do due diligence to your market research.

- **Book subtitle:** If you already have your title, consider using keyword strings in your subtitle to help boost your exposure in searches. And consider whether you want to put your subtitle on your book cover. Leaving it off makes it a lot easier to change it on Amazon to match market needs and industry and genre trends.

- **Book topic:** Let's say you're an expert in your field but aren't sure what topic to write about. Let's say you're a consumer finance guru and want to write a book on this topic. Knowing what consumers are searching for in the area of finance, and what keyword strings are used most often, is a great way to home in on the immediate needs of your readers. Create a topic that's narrower. Instead of addressing a broad area, tighten your focus. It will net you better sales. Consumers like specialized topics that help solve specific problems. And the books don't have to be long. Once you find your market or niche, you'll want to publish regularly for your target audience.

Now, let's assume you've done the keyword string research suggested in this book. Let's see how these searches relate to popular topics on Amazon.

Give this a try:

1. On the Amazon page, search the Kindle store tab. Isolate your searches there for now.

2. Plug in your search term and see what comes up. You'll generally get five to ten suggestions. Click on one of them.

3. Look at the books that come up in the search and click on the "Customers Also Bought" section.

4. Focus on books with a high sales rank. Depending on the category, it could be between 50,000 and 20,000.

5. Make sure there are a variety of books in the Also Bought section, preferably more than five around the same topic, and make sure that they all have this range of sales volume. If it's lower than 20,000, that's great, but neither the super-saturated nor the unpopular categories will help you.

Some Amazon experts say a 20,000 rank indicates the book is selling five copies a day, but I find this hard to prove either way. Just know that, given Amazon's volume, a book is definitely not languishing at that rank.

In addition to topic research, while you're developing your book idea and trying to decide what to include and exclude, consider spending a bit of time comparing the content of similar books in your market. Take advantage of Amazon's "look inside" book feature and read several pages, as well as the reviews. Readers will tell you what they want, and they'll often do it in a review. The negative reviews with constructive feedback—those that explain what readers thought was missing or things they wished had been expanded upon—will be especially helpful.

STAYING ON THE SHORT AND NARROW

While full-length books will never go away, there's a trend toward shorter, niche books—books that "own" a narrow market segment. This is also a smart strategy for stretching your knowledge across multiple products, because remember, rarely will one title help you reach your author or business goals.

When I first published *How to Sell Books by the Truckload on Amazon*, I was surprised at how its sales outpaced my other books. While I know the title had a lot to do with this, the book was also shorter and more tightly focused on one particular area.

Keep in mind that if you do short, you don't have room for fluff. You'll want to be crystal clear and feature specific instructions, maybe even including step-by-step instructions or checklists, which readers love.

How short can short be? 10,000 to 17,000 words is generally acceptable. Anything under 50 pages is too short; 65 pages is a safe bet but be cautious when you format your final contents. If your book has too few pages, Amazon's "look inside" feature will reveal most of the content, or enough that readers may glean what they want and not buy it. This is where a thorough (and often longer and more detailed) table of contents comes in very handy—it creates a good snapshot of what's inside your book, without giving away the store.

If you've finished the book and it still seems a bit too short, consider adding things like checklists, free resources, or bonus chapters from other books you've written that relate to the topic. Beware, don't plump up your page count just to plump it up! Make sure you're adding helpful, useful, relevant information. If the book has too much white paper instead of text, you may end up with a lot of window-shoppers who don't end up buying. And while short is the new long, if you do decide to write shorter books, don't be exclusive about it. Mixing it up is the best route to success.

SIMPLE KEYWORD STRING SUCCESS STRATEGIES TO ROCK YOUR BOOK

Now that you understand where your keyword strings come into play in the context of your Amazon back-end, behind-the-scenes information, let's take a more comprehensive look at the other ways you can use keyword strings.

TITLES AND SUBTITLES

A book's title can often make or break its success, but most authors fail to consider adding keywords strings to their title and/or subtitle. Many times, particularly in nonfiction, I see authors give their books nebulous titles. This is a mistake, especially when you consider all the titles on Amazon and all of the books your reader has to choose from. If you've written nonfiction, be as benefit-driven and as specific as you can be.

Some of you are probably thinking you've missed the boat because your book is already out, but you haven't!

Whether or not you've already published your book, there are some key strategies pertaining to subtitles that can really benefit you. Keep in mind that these examples are for fiction, and I chose fiction intentionally. Fiction tends to be a tougher market to use keyword strings in the subtitle, and certainly in the title. But take a look at what some fiction authors are doing, and I'm sure it'll spark some great ideas, regardless of your genre or niche.

USING DESCRIPTIVE SUBTITLES

Some fiction books put their descriptive subtitles right on the cover. That means the author did their research in advance and knew what their dramatic hook was at the time their cover was being created. Take a look at these examples:

Spring at Blueberry Bay: An utterly perfect feel good romantic comedy Kindle Edition

by Holly Martin

Welcome to beautiful Hope Island where the sea sparkles, the daffodils are blooming and a blossoming romance is just around the corner...

Bella has always had a sunny outlook and caring nature, despite recently falling on hard times. When she finds a handsome homeless man on her doorstep, her kind heart tells her she must help him. So,...

You can also create a descriptive subtitle after your book cover has been designed by simply adding a subtitle on the back end of Amazon. Here's an example of a great subtitle that isn't listed on the book's cover.

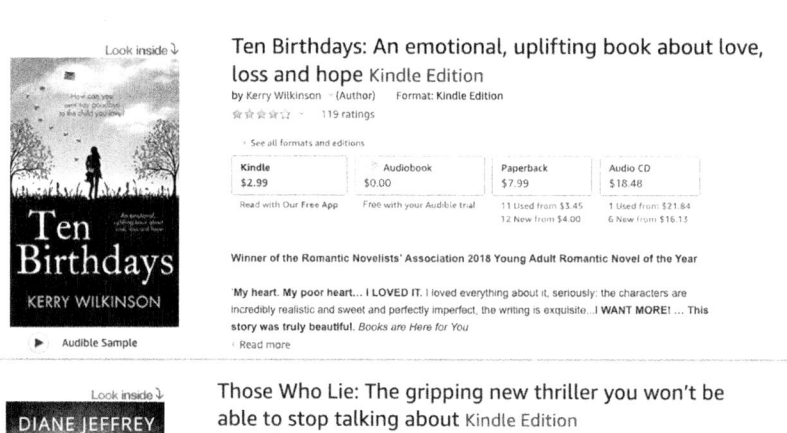

Ten Birthdays: An emotional, uplifting book about love, loss and hope Kindle Edition

by Kerry Wilkinson

Winner of the Romantic Novelists' Association 2018 Young Adult Romantic Novel of the Year

'My heart. My poor heart... I LOVED IT. I loved everything about it, seriously: the characters are incredibly realistic and sweet and perfectly imperfect, the writing is exquisite...I WANT MORE! ... This story was truly beautiful.' *Books are Here for You*

Those Who Lie: The gripping new thriller you won't be able to stop talking about Kindle Edition

by Diane Jeffrey

'[A] scorchingly good thriller' – Lisa Hall, bestselling author of mega-hit *Between You and Me*

'A tantalising and taut thriller with more twists and turns than a corkscrew. Red herrings swim all the way through it. An excellent page turner' – Sally (Goodreads)

Emily Klein doesn't know she has killed her husband until the day of

SIMPLE KEYWORD STRING SUCCESS STRATEGIES TO ROCK YOUR BOOK | 35

Also, subtitles help to differentiate your book on search pages, too. Have a look:

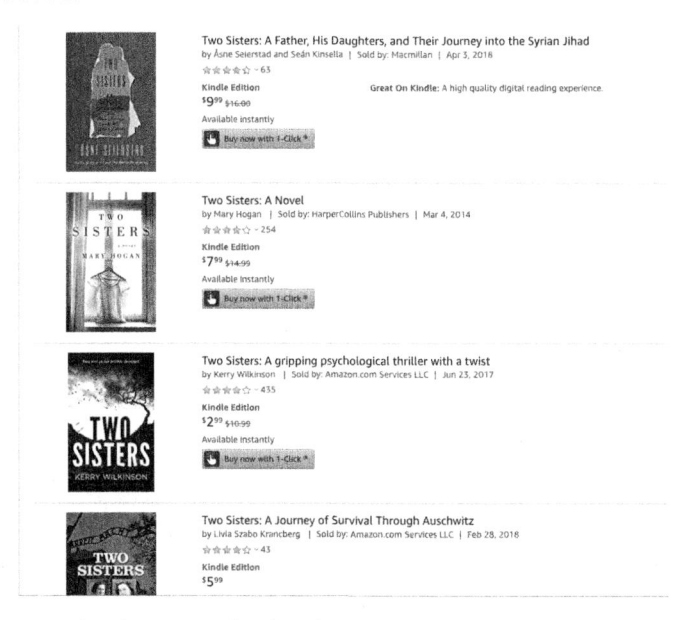

These subtitles give the books a very effective descriptive boost. With so much popping up on Amazon intended to distract readers and draw their attention to other products, it's smart to assume readers no longer spend a lot of time reading book descriptions, and vague, "guess what this book is about" book titles just don't work anymore. Now the majority of browsing time is spent with the cover image, title, and subtitle. You can see how each subtitle above helps further enhance the page while also speaking to the reader's particular goal in finding the right book.

Adding a subtitle on the cover is fine, but keep in mind that if you're sitting in a genre where reader preferences and keyword strings change frequently, you may want to avoid doing that. An example of this might be in the romance genre, where trends tend to change frequently. You also have to consider what you're committing to when you put your subtitle on your cover. Perhaps your reviews will prove readers are getting something entirely different from your book that you hadn't considered, and when that happens, you can update your subtitle on Amazon but you're stuck with what you chose for your cover.

USING KEYWORD STRINGS FROM YOUR METADATA

As we discussed earlier in this book, good keyword strings for your Amazon page are crucial. But these Amazon keywords can also be used in your subtitle, too. This is why having a subtitle on a book can be good, but also not so good, as I pointed out earlier.

The trick with a good subtitle is that you want something that isn't simply a crammed-together collection of keywords. It needs to make sense as well. In other cases, you want to make sure you're appealing to your reader and what will attract them. For example, using the term, "Clean romance" or "Fast-paced thriller," can help get the attention of key readers. Something like this works:

A Royal Affair Series: Book 1, 2, and 3: A time travel, royal romance Kindle Edition
by Christina George (Author)   Format: Kindle Edition
108 ratings

See all formats and editions

Kindle	Paperback
$4.95	$15.95
Read with Our Free App	1 Used from $8.95 1 New from $15.95

Before Harry and Meghan, there was the fairytale love story of Peter and Emma...

What if the love of your life lived 200 years ago?

This next book would probably benefit from a subtitle more geared to pulling in new readers. If you aren't familiar with who Poppy McVie is, you might not be inclined to click on the "buy" button.

The following example has a great, fun cover as well, but no subtitle, which I think could certainly help improve sales.

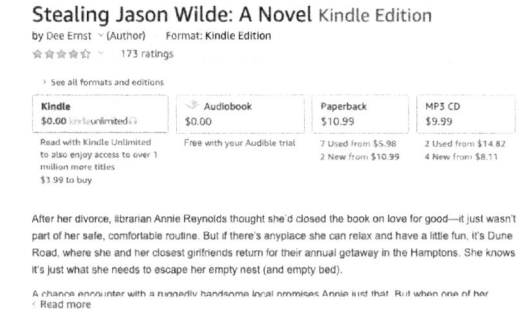

BOOK DESCRIPTION

The book description, often overlooked as a means to drive traffic to your page, is also a great place to use keywords and keyword strings. A book description should draw the reader in, but authors tend to be too close to their own work to write an objective description that dances along the line between saying just enough but not revealing so much it gets too wordy or overly complex-sounding.

Here's a screenshot of the product page for the book, *How to Sell a Truckload of Books on Amazon*. Notice that I use keyword strings throughout the page—in the header, in the description, and in the bullets:

"I've been at this for 43 years now and your two little books are, quite seriously, the best and most 'user friendly' I've seen on the subject of book marketing in all that time."

Jim Cox, Midwest Book Review

Learn How to Turn Amazon into your 24/7 Book Sales Machine!

Selling books can often be a confusing process, but How to Sell Books by the Truckload on Amazon (2020 edition) teaches you exactly how to do it – but smarter and with more success.

Named as one of the top influencers of 2019 by New York Metropolitan Magazine, Penny Sansevieri has also taught Amazon-centric classes and webinars to thousands of authors leading up to the release of this **ultimate guide** to mastering the Amazon marketing system. Follow her proven strategies and you'll immediately start building your book's target market exposure and dramatically upgrade your overall book marketing efforts!Don't waste time with all the misinformation out there, instead, let Penny Sansevieri show you how to:

When it comes to fiction, the rules still apply, but you may have to be creative in using your keyword strings. Let's say you find a series of keyword strings like this:

- new romance eBooks
- romance and sex
- romance eBooks
- romance and mystery

It's pretty tough to fit these into a general description if you're sharing things like character details and theme, but you should consider using descriptors that include important keyword strings. Or, if you've already used a subtitle, you should also figure out a creative way to repeat it in the book description. If your book description is long enough, you could definitely include some keywords. Be careful of using a longer keyword string, such as, "Best new romance eBook," because it will look awkward and self-aggrandizing.

Instead, consider incorporating a phrase as an additional descriptor in review quotes—*but only if you check with your reviewer/endorser for permission and approval of your rewrite*. For example:

> **"Loved this book…packed with romance and sex!"**
>
> **"Fantastic buy and among one of the best new romance eBooks!"**

Do not fail to check with your endorser and ask if it's okay if the review is reworded slightly. Don't redo the entire review; ideally, you should only have to add a word or two to weave in the keyword strings.

Something I've done is add them after the review. If someone writes, "This is a thrill-a-minute ride. I couldn't put it down!" I add, "Sally Reviewer, commenting on this romance and mystery book." It has the potential to look somewhat awkward, so you'll want to play around with it until it feels and reads right. The bottom line is, weaving in as many keyword phrases/strings as possible can substantially improve your search rank.

Some SEO experts will tell you to use just one string, while others say you should cram all of them into your description. For nonfiction, this is pretty simple. Fiction is trickier. Use what feels and reads right; don't overstuff your description just for the sake of inserting keyword strings.

I read a book about Amazon promotion that said you should use your keywords seven times. Frankly, I don't think the number of times matters. It's the nature of the keywords that matters, so spend your time creating a description that utilizes these terms and presents your book in the best possible light. My sense is that, much like the use of author names in keyword strings, Amazon will start cracking down on keyword-stuffing in the book description, too—so be careful!

UNDERSTANDING AMAZON ENHANCED CATEGORIES

Your book's categories are extremely important. They're so much more than simply where your audience will find the book. The more niched, the more specific you can get, the better. This is why I refer to categories as "enhanced," because that's exactly what we're going to dig into in this chapter.

The reality is this: the narrower your category, the better you'll do on Amazon overall. Much of this has to do with the way the algorithm works. Some nonfiction authors look at bigger categories, like business or self-help, and think, "I want to dominate that category!" That is a great goal, but it's often not realistic. If you can dominate a smaller niche category, it will trigger Amazon algorithms, which in turn triggers their internal promotion system.

On Amazon, sales breed sales. The more sales you get, the more sales Amazon wants you to get. Digging into niche categories can be another way to trigger this system.

Keep in mind that Amazon is divided into two websites, the main book site and the Kindle store. If you're only doing category research on the main book site, you may be missing out on some great possibilities. My preference is to only do category research in the Amazon Kindle store. Why? Because there are so many new books being published on Amazon, many of them in Kindle format, which tend to have more variety and better, more narrow results.

Amazon has also changed how many categories you can have. Originally you were allowed to have four, then Amazon dropped it to two. Now you're allowed to have *ten categories!* Why would you want ten? Because it's a great way to get in front of more readers. It's a bit like seeing Starbucks on almost every corner. If you're craving a cup of coffee or a quick bite, you're more likely to go to a Starbucks since they're literally everywhere. The same is true when your book is in multiple categories. It'll show up in more places, in more searches. You get the idea.

With ten categories to work with, you may have to balance between very niche categories and broader ones. Yes, I said that niche categories are a must—and they are. But if you're trying to get into ten categories, you're bound to find one or two that aren't as narrow as you'd like. That's totally fine. I'd rather be in ten areas, even if a couple are a long shot, than sell my book short on opportunities.

When you're trying to decide which categories make the most sense, it helps to think outside your core market. For example, if you've written a business or nutrition book, instead of leaving the book in "Business" or "Dieting," two super-huge categories on Amazon, you'll want to put it into something slightly narrower, like the subcategory "Women and Business," or "Macrobiotics." to help make sure it won't get lost in the onslaught of books dominating these markets. I'll address this again, in more depth, in a few pages.

You may also want to mix up your markets, consider what other areas your book might do well in. For example, I have a book called *Red Hot Internet Publicity*, which I put in both the "Business" and "Internet Marketing" sections. Readers might search both areas, so I'm covered.

Be aware that categories can change, and often do—and without notice. Sometimes Amazon even deletes categories. It won't delete your book from the system, but it will delete it from that category—and arbitrarily put it somewhere else.

FINDING THE BEST CATEGORIES ON AMAZON

The Kindle side of Amazon has some great additional categories for your book. Here's how to access it:

1. Go to the Amazon.com search bar and highlight Kindle Store, as in the screenshot below:

2. Then click Go, but do not put a book title in the search bar. Highlighting Kindle Store and clicking Go will drop you into the Kindle side of Amazon, which has a whole different set of categories.

3. Once you're there, click on Kindle eBooks, and voilà, now you can really start digging around. The key here is to keep clicking that bar to the left (see image below) until you find some good places to put your book. Again, you may not always strike gold with categories that have only 320 books in them, but you'll find many great ones where you can easily add your book!

```
< Kindle Store
  Kindle eBooks
    Arts & Photography
    Biographies & Memoirs
    Business & Money
    Children's eBooks
    Comics, Manga & Graphic Novels
    Computers & Technology
    Cookbooks, Food & Wine
    Crafts, Hobbies & Home
    Education & Teaching
    Engineering & Transportation
    Foreign Languages
    Health, Fitness & Dieting
    History
    Humor & Entertainment
    Law
    Lesbian, Gay, Bisexual & Transgender eBooks
    Literature & Fiction
    Medical eBooks
    Mystery, Thriller & Suspense
    Nonfiction
    Parenting & Relationships
    Politics & Social Sciences
    Reference
    Religion & Spirituality
    Romance
    Science & Math
    Science Fiction & Fantasy
    Self-Help
    Sports & Outdoors
    Teen & Young Adult
    Travel
```

CHANGING YOUR CATEGORIES ON AMAZON

When you first publish on Amazon or add your book to their system, they will ask you for the categories where you want your book listed. These are standard industry categories, called BISAC—used by everyone from bookstores to specialty stores. Your categories for your eBook will be different, and we'll discuss those in a minute. When you first upload your print and eBook to the system, you'll be stuck with the standard industry categories until you change them. Now let's look at how you can make those changes.

When you've found the right category for your eBook in the Kindle store, you'll want to make sure that your book is added to it. You can do this by emailing the links for the categories to Amazon via the Author Central portal. Log into your Author Central account via: authorcentral.amazon.com. If you've never accessed this portal, just use your Amazon username and password. Once you're in there, click on Help. After you click on Help, select Contact Us. Once you get there, you'll click the following in this order:

- My Books

- Update information about a book

- Browse categories

- I want to update my book's browse categories

If you're still unsure and haven't spent a lot of time on the Amazon platform, check out my Master Amazon and Sell More Books Membership. You'll find a number of videos where I show you step-by-step how to navigate Amazon and work with their customer service to get the additional help you need!

REFINE: BY THEMES FOR FICTION

According to Amazon, their refine-by section was implemented for fiction because consumers were searching for things like the type of protagonist or setting (beach, city, etc.).

What are refine-by themes?

Refine-by themes are, in general, various aspects of your book's content. For example, if you have a wealthy protagonist, one of your themes would be "Wealthy." If you have a murder mystery with a serial killer, your theme might be "Serial killer." Here's what themes look like on the romance side of the Amazon page:

You can see a list of "Romantic Themes" and "Romantic Heroes" on the left-hand side of the screen. If you've written a thriller or mystery, you'll have three choices: "Moods & Themes," "Characters," and "Setting."

How do you use refine-by themes in your Amazon strategy?

You'll want test adding refine-by keywords to your other keyword strings and qualify them the same way you do other keywords, by checking their supply and demand. Not all of them will work, mind you. Some are just too specific, and while readers are interested in books in these niche categories, if they're not using those exact words in searches, it won't help you. However, some refine-bys are easy to incorporate and often produce positive results—like adding "dark" to an already solid keyword string for a thriller or suspense book—and you should take advantage of these easy wins.

Keyword qualifying is not a quick and easy strategy to master, but practice makes perfect.

If you're interested in finding out how to do it better, take advantage of the discount code to my Master Amazon and Sell More Books Video Membership listed at the end of the book!

HOW TO ACHIEVE MORE VISIBILITY FOR OBSCURE OR NICHE BOOKS

What if you've published a book that has a limited audience due to a topic which isn't widely known? How do you drive attention to a book about something that doesn't enjoy popular awareness? The good news is, it's totally possible—and I'm going to tell you how!

Consider the steam mop. Ever heard of it? If not, you may want to get one. Unless you want to keep cleaning your floors with a regular mop that doesn't kill germs. Who wants that? Did you know you can also clean carpets *and* rugs with a steam mop?

See what I did there? I got you to go from "What the heck is a steam mop?" to "Well, yeah, I want to keep my floors germ-free!"

The idea here is that you need alignment, and that's where your keyword strings can take you. Alignment is the concept of bringing together two ideas that aren't obviously related and then connecting them to sell your idea—in this case, your book.

First you will need to find out "where it hurts," or what the problem is that needs to be solved.

Recently I was doing an Amazon optimization for a book about better breathing, in other words, how to oxygenate your blood better. This is an interesting market because it's big, I mean we all breathe. But it's also deceptive, because most consumers don't head over to Amazon to learn how to breathe better. The upside for an author is that there aren't a lot of breathing books on Amazon.

Reduced competition sounds great, right? In reality, especially Amazon reality, it's not so great in this case, because the books already on Amazon related to this book on breathing, had very high sales rankings. There may be less competition, but the competition could be very stiff!

While I was working on this optimization, I decided to go after different reasons someone might buy this book, for example if you're feeling tired, or you suffer from brain fog—a book about breathing better could be helpful. The same is true for losing weight (I found this one surprising) better breathing can also help with weight loss. The end result was a set of keyword strings that tied the book to those issues. Once we did that, this author was able to boost the overall bounce of the book on Amazon and get it in front of readers who might want to consider other options for dealing with fatigue, weight loss, memory, brain fog—the list is really endless.

The thing about this strategy—and this is specific to nonfiction—is that you need to make sure your book description matches and is aligned with this train of thought. In the case of the breathing book, I suggested she update the book description to include these benefits better breathing can offer, which matched the keywords and categories I found, too.

I followed this same process with a book about a memoir of a husband's suicide due to a drug addiction. Memoirs are generally a tougher market anyway, so I'll always try to anchor them to a bigger, broader message. In general, suicide is a tough thing to market. However drug addiction in this country is a massive problem, and sadly, something that a lot of people can relate to, so that's where I focused my optimization efforts. I found channels, along with memoir and suicide, that the book would fit into and could also pull in readers that had dealt with addiction in a family member.

The goal in a category with low competition is a higher sales ranking which translates to selling a ton of books—which is golden!

Additionally, I recommended to this author that she remove all references to death and suicide from her keyword strings and instead focus on addiction, drug addiction, memoir and the like—because suicide isn't something that's heavily searched on Amazon. Remember, the underlying factors for the outcome are what you're looking to align your book with.

The key idea is to make your book the end of the road in terms of readers' needs. Show them that whether they want to be entertained, educated, or enlightened, your book is what they need.

However, in order to get them there, you have to help them find the path to discovery with the correct keyword strings, book descriptions, and categories.

Most authors fail at this and instead, make choices that are too broad and therefore, lose opportunities for readers to find them.

If you can reach them earlier, you can present your book without a huge crowd of competing distractions and gain new readers. You'll be surprised how well this works.

And while it's a tad less obvious, the same is true for boosting visibility of any fiction book. Tying your book to ideas your readers may be interested in—paranormal elements, specific settings, or other book attributes, can help you gain more real estate in those vital search areas.

HOW GREAT AMAZON BOOK DESCRIPTIONS HELP INDIE AUTHORS SELL MORE BOOKS

Whether we're talking about Amazon or any other online retailer, book descriptions are more important than most authors realize.

Too often I see simple details overlooked that can really make or break an author's ability to turn an Amazon browser into their next book buyer.

In this section we'll discuss some ideas about book descriptions specifically, and then review some tips you may want to consider in order to enhance your own book description for maximum effectiveness on Amazon.

SCANNING VERSUS READING

Most people don't read websites, they scan. The same is true for your book description. If you have huge blocks of text without any consideration for spacing, boldface, bulleted lists, short paragraphs, or some other form of highlighting that helps the reader scan and zero in on the best of the best you have to offer, it's unlikely to attract readers. When your description is visually and psychologically appealing, it invites the reader to keep going, instead of clicking to a different page.

Book design, meaning the actual font on the pages, should also be visually appealing. By having wide margins (referred to as gutters in the book design world) and spacing, and, in nonfiction, bulleted lists and even boxed-in pieces to highlight particular text, you encourage the reader to take in all of your content, instead of doing a quick scan and rushing on.

Our minds are image processors, not text processors, so huge pieces of text that fill a page overwhelm the mind and, in fact, slow down the processing time considerably.

When we're looking at websites, our attention span is even shorter than it is while reading a book. Even sites like Amazon—where consumers go to buy, and often spend a lot of time comparing products and reading reviews—it's important to keep in mind that most potential readers will move on if your description is too cumbersome.

MAKING YOUR DESCRIPTION MORE SCAN-FRIENDLY

- **Headlines:** The first sentence in the description should be a grabber, something that pulls the reader in. This text could also be an excerpt of an enthusiastic review or some other kind of endorsement, but regardless, it should be bolded.

- **Paragraphs:** Keep paragraphs short, 2-3 sentences max, and let some powerful sentences stand on their own.

- **Bolding and Italics:** You can boldface key text throughout the description. In fact, I recommend it. Just be sure you aren't using boldface or italics too much. It'll have more impact if you do just one sentence or a few keyword strings.

- **Bullets or Numbers:** If your book is nonfiction, it can be very effective to bullet or number as much of your information as possible. Take key points and the "here's what you'll learn" elements and put them into a bullet point/numbering section that's easy to scan and visually appealing.

USE CODE TO ENHANCE YOUR AMAZON BOOK DESCRIPTION AND HEADLINE

How do you spruce up the text styles within your book description? There are several types of code you can use to enhance your headline and description. Keep in mind that you can't make these changes to your headline via Author Central; it all has to be done from the KDP Dashboard. Although this won't affect your algorithm per se, it will help make your book description more visually appealing.

Here are some of the coding enhancers available:

Bolding: The text you want bolded
Italics: <i>The text you want italicized</i>
Headline: <h1>The text you want for a headline</h1>
Numbered list:
<ol>
<li>First sentence</li>
<li>Second sentence</li>
<li>Third sentence</li>
</ol>
For a bulleted list just change the <ol> to <ul>.

ANSWERING "WHAT'S IN IT FOR ME?"

The biggest challenge authors face is writing a book description that effectively highlights the book's benefits for readers. This matters whether it's fiction or nonfiction, and it's a crucial part of any book description.

Remember, with 4,500+ books published *every day* in this country, you can't afford to have a vague, meandering book description. You must state clearly why your book is the best one they can buy.

This leads us to the differences between fiction and nonfiction when it comes to book descriptions.

NONFICTION

First off, it's probably very likely that whomever you're targeting already owns a few titles similar to the one you just wrote. Then why on earth should they add yours to their collection?

While you're powering through your book description, keep in mind that you're likely serving a very cluttered market. Yes, you should feel confident you have a unique point of view, but they'll never know that if your book description isn't doing its job.

You need to be precise and vividly clear about why your book matters. You should both hook the reader from the first sentence, and make a personal connection to the reader via the book description.

Nonfiction shoppers are more often than not looking for the solution to a problem. They're not browsing for their next beach read, so your book description needs to *zero in on what that problem is*. Also, readers need to feel like you understand them, and be convinced you're the best person to help them work through their problem.

If you're a noted expert in your field, with accolades to back it up, work those in briefly, because in this day and age it truly does set you apart. Definitely use reviews by other experts in your field or industry but keep them short and sweet—excerpts of the best parts are plenty. Save your full bio and complete reviews for the other sections Amazon gives you.

FICTION

Fiction is a bit tougher, because it's easy to reveal too much, or not quite enough. For this reason, I encourage you to focus on developing your elevator pitch (see below), because that's going to be your cliffhanger, or your readers' key interest point in the book. Every other piece of the story anchors to that.

When it comes to fiction, buyers have a lot of options, so be clear about what your book is about, and lead with the hook. Your opening sentence should be the best you've got—it might be the only chance you get. Don't confuse not giving it all away with being vague. If you're vague, you can't convince the potential reader your book fits the genre they're interested in. They won't experience the emotional connection that is necessary in order to make them want to know more. Give them a story arc to latch onto which will leave them wanting more.

Keep movie trailers in mind while you're writing your fiction description. They often do an outstanding job of revealing enough of the story to get readers hooked, without bogging them down with too many details they can't appreciate yet, or without revealing so much that it prevents them from watching it.

CHILDREN'S AND/OR YOUNG ADULT TITLES

For these books, make sure to include the intended age range. Even though you can add it in the Amazon details, I've had parents tell me that seeing it in the book description is incredibly helpful, because if anyone is short on time and needs help making smart buying decisions, it's parents.

It also helps a lot to let them know right away what their child will learn, or what discussions or themes the book will highlight. Remember, while you wrote the book for children, you're selling it to adults, so don't oversimplify your description, thinking you're off the hook. Adjust your approach to reach parents who are short on time. They'll buy the book that leaves very little room for error—something that seems like a sure thing.

DEVELOPING YOUR ELEVATOR PITCH

What is an elevator pitch, and why do you need one?

An elevator pitch is a one- to two-sentence description of your book. It's the briefest of the brief descriptions you will develop. Elevator pitches are important because we have ever-shrinking attention spans, and there are times when you need to capture someone's attention with a very short, succinct pitch.

Why does this matter for your book description?

Because having a short hook is an excellent way to start building your book description. Also, elevator pitches focus on the core of your book—the one element that your book could not be without—and that's what matters most to your reader.

Keep Your Wording Simple

When it comes to writing a book description, I encourage you to save your five-dollar words for another time. Book descriptions that work well tend to use simple language that any layperson can understand. If you make someone pause to think about a word, you'll lose them.

Don't underestimate the power of a thesaurus. While you may want to repeat a few lucrative keyword strings, you don't want too much repetition because it will get boring. Great public speakers don't use the same words over and over again, because they understand the importance of creating good sound bites, and they're smart about choosing words that aren't overused. This is a winning strategy for creating something memorable that stands out from the competition.

HOW EXCITED ARE YOU?
AND HOW EXCITED WILL YOUR READERS BE?

Have you ever seen a book description with a ton of exclamation points or all caps? Like an email, it feels as if the writer is screaming at you.

Although I don't recommend eliminating exclamation points entirely from your book description, they should be used sparingly. I'd recommend one or two at most. An exclamation point used here and there can help make a sentence seem even more emphatic.

In terms of all caps, don't even bother. Using all caps, even for a word or two or a single sentence in a book description, makes you look like an amateur.

SPELL CHECK

Using spell check should go without saying, yet I've still seen enough descriptions loaded with typos that I feel like I need to say it. Please don't put up a book description full of typos. Even one is too many. Have a friend or colleague read it for you before you put it on Amazon, and again as soon as it's live—and then make edits ASAP.

IS YOUR BOOK PART OF A SERIES?

Fiction readers love a series. Tell them right up front that your book is part of an ongoing story or theme. Many readers are specifically searching for a great series when they come to Amazon. Add it right in the headline. I also recommend that you make it part of the title, too. For example, you might word your book title like this: *Deadly Heat: Heat Series, Book 4 of 7.*

Here's an example of Dan Silva's book title, which is a good illustration of putting series information in the actual book title:

The Black Widow (Gabriel Allon Series Book 16) Kindle Edition
by Daniel Silva (Author)   Format: Kindle Edition

INCLUDE TOP KEYWORDS

Keywords are as important to your Amazon book page as almost anything else. I've created a number of videos as part of my Master Amazon and Sell More Books Membership, but here's a quick overview:

The term "keyword" is actually inaccurate, because readers don't search based on a single keyword. Think instead of keyword strings.

For example, "Romance about second chances" or "Second-chance romances," have been popular search strings on Amazon for a while now. However, by taking that sentence and inserting it into your book description, you can help boost your visibility on the site, as well as keying into your readers' specific interest. If they're searching for, "Romance second chances," and they see it in your book description, it's going to ping them with: "Oh! This is exactly the book I've been looking for."

That said, it's a good idea to avoid overstuffing your book description with keywords. I recommend using them if you can keep it natural, but don't sacrifice a better description just to include more keywords.

DON'T MARKET TO YOUR EGO

I often say to authors, "No one cares that you wrote a book." And while family and friends may care, they aren't your target audience. If you want to pull in readers—a lot of them—make sure your book appeals to *their* needs and *their* interests, not *yours*. If you're unsure about whether or not you've pulled this off, do a reader profile brainstorm, or buyer market analysis to ensure you're fully fleshed out about who your readers are and what makes them tick. You won't regret it, because this kind of knowledge is useful across the board in many facets of your promotion.

INCLUDE REVIEWS AND REWARDS

If you earned a stand-out review from a professional reviewer or book blogger, or if you won an award, be sure to highlight it in your description. Be smart about using the best of the best though, and use excerpts instead of full quotes.

GET A SECOND OPINION

We're often too close to our own work to fully wrap our minds around what the market wants from us. From my own experience, I can tell you it's a delicate balance between teaching authors what I feel they need to learn and discussing problems they want me to address.

I'd strongly encourage you to use your editor's help for your book's description, or get some feedback from other trusted individuals who know your market really well, and take their suggestions and edits to heart.

UPDATE YOUR PAGE OFTEN

This is something you may not have considered: Your page isn't set in cement. In fact, ideally it shouldn't be static. When you get good reviews and awards, update your book page to reflect that. When you do your keyword string and category research every quarter (yep, put it on the list) consider whether there are any new ones you can sprinkle throughout the different sections on Author Central.

Here's another idea. If you're doing a special promotion, book promo, discount, or whatever, why not mention it in your book description? (See screenshot below.)

I worked with a client this year who did a special bonus download on her website during the book's preorder period, and I encouraged her to highlight it on her book description to drive even more engagements and downloads.

Finally, take a look at the book description below from Dan Silva. It's a good example of a blurb that combines great review quotes with a book description that pulls you in from the first sentence.

Book reviews are eye candy, because people like what other people like. Even if you don't have review quotes from highly respected or recognizable publications such as *Booklist* and *Publishers Weekly*, you should still add reviews. Just be sure to cite them correctly.

Notice how they are boldfaced to draw attention to them? And check out the second paragraph. Whoever wrote this book description inserted a review to help bolster the character description, which is another clever idea.

> **"Fascinating, suspenseful, and bated-breath exciting.... Silva proves once again that he can rework familiar genre material and bring it to new life."**
> — *Publishers Weekly*, starred review
>
> **"Silva builds suspense like a symphony conductor.... A winner on all fronts."**
> — *Booklist*, starred review
>
> Bestselling author Daniel Silva delivers another spellbinding international thriller—one that finds the legendary Gabriel Allon grappling with an ISIS mastermind.
>
> Gabriel Allon, the art restorer, spy, and assassin described as the most compelling fictional creation "since Ian Fleming put down his martini and invented James Bond" (*Rocky Mountain News*), is poised to become the chief of Israel's secret intelligence service. But on the eve of his promotion, events conspire to lure him into the field for one final operation. ISIS has detonated a massive bomb in the Marais district of Paris, and a desperate French government wants Gabriel to eliminate the man responsible before he can strike again.

Book descriptions are your sales pitch. And ultimately, descriptions will or won't sell your book, so make sure yours is tightly written, exceptionally engaging, and most of all, turns a browser into a buyer.

HOW TO WRITE A KICK-ASS AMAZON BIO TO SELL MORE BOOKS

Authors often don't spend enough time crafting their bios. Most of them write up a quick "about me" to satisfy the basic requirements and never give it a second thought. I often see authors treat their bio like a resume, and risk boring readers to death, or they treat it like a throwaway and totally miss that it makes them look not only less interesting, but less interested in their own work and how they're coming across to readers.

Have I hit a nerve? Good!

Unless you tell me that you know for a fact your bio is helping turn more browsers into buyers, I know for a fact I can help you make it better!

START WITH AN OUTLINE AND ALL BOOK TIE-INS

Before you begin, create a list or an outline of everything you've done related to the book. This can include life experiences, personal motivations, passion projects, research, past work in a related industry, accreditations, lectures and classes you've conducted, other books you've written, and awards you've won. You may want to include some of these elements, but not all of them. The rest of these bullets will help you determine which to include.

BUT IT'S NOT REALLY ABOUT YOU

Remember that while we start out by focusing on you and your achievements, this bio actually isn't about you. It's about your reader and knowing what your prospective audience is looking for, what interests them, what catches their attention, and most importantly, what speaks to their needs.

Let's take a close look at a bio on Amazon by author, Mark Shaefer. His bio is keenly focused on his expertise as it relates to the book. Having read Mark's other books and having seen him speak, I can tell you he probably has a lot more he could have added to this, but he kept it short and relevant to the book.

About the Author

Mark W. Schaefer is a globally-recognized author, speaker, educator, and business consultant who blogs at {grow} - one of the top marketing blogs of the world. He teaches graduate marketing classes at Rutgers University and has written four best-selling books including The Tao of Twitter (the best-selling book on Twitter in the world) and Return On Influence, which was named one of the top business titles of the year by the American Library Association. His clients include Dell, Adidas, and the US Air Force. He has been a keynote speaker at prestigious events all over the world including SXSW, Marketing Summit Tokyo, and the Institute for International and European Affairs.

WRITE IN THIRD PERSON

When it comes to writing a bio, never use words like "I" and "me," because a bio written in the first person can make for an awkward read, especially when running through your accomplishments. There are other options for getting personal, don't worry!

SHOW THE READER YOUR EXPERTISE WITHOUT THE EGO

When it comes to the credible portion of the bio you are creating or reworking, this may seem tricky. But remember, this is where the importance of your initial work comes in. How long have you been writing? Did you utilize any special techniques or resources in this book?

Check out Pete Ryan's bio. He's a first-time author, but he leads this bio with his background as a journalist, which tells the reader he is an experienced writer. Pete is also a marketing guy and has a successful business in So Cal. You'll notice he doesn't even mention it, because it won't matter to his fiction readers, and Pete knows this.

› Visit Amazon's Peter J. Ryan Page

Biography

Peter J. Ryan spent years as a journalist before venturing into the wilds of fiction writing. EDGE OF THE SAWTOOTH is his first novel. A tireless backcountry hiker and overall outdoor enthusiast, Ryan splits his time between Huntington Beach, California, and Paradise Valley, Montana. He is married with four grown children and three grandchildren. For more information visit www.peterjryan.net.

‹ Follow

ADD KEYWORD STRINGS PARTICULAR TO AMAZON

As you already know, keyword strings matter greatly on Amazon. If you've already done your keyword string research, work some into your Amazon bio if you can keep it natural.

Don't cram your bio full of keywords just for the sake of having them there.

Why does this matter? I've talked about how Amazon is a search engine. Like a search engine, Amazon will "spider" or "crawl" our book page for keyword strings, so make sure at least one or two of the ones you've found are in your bio, but don't overdo it because you'll get dinged by readers for being inauthentic.

BE PERSONAL (IF APPROPRIATE)

There's a time and a place to include personal information in your bio. Memoir of course, self-help, genres where your connection to the topic is crucial. But fiction authors can also get personal in a creative way, because your personality says a lot about your brand.

The key is finding the right balance. For example, if you write paranormal fantasy, the fact that you coach your daughter's softball team may sound endearing, but it doesn't fit your genre. Though if you've always had a fascination with mythology and history, and it fuels your stories, that's great insight into who you are.

BE FUNNY (IF APPROPRIATE)

Be like what you wrote about. That means if your book is funny, then be funny. Check out this bio from Karen Alpert. Her book is *I Heart My Little A-Holes: A bunch of holy-crap moments no one ever told you about parenting*.

Amazon.com Review

Karen Alpert
There are a Lot of Reasons I Wrote This Book, I Mean, Besides Money by Karen Alpert

When I had my daughter I remember looking down at my newborn and thinking there's a reason God made babies ridiculously cute. So we wouldn't give them away. Or eat them. Because having a kid is like the hardest thing on earth. I mean yeah it's super rewarding and you can't help but loving them to pieces, but no one ever tells you before you have kids just how difficult it's going to be.

And you'd never know it from looking at Facebook or Pinterest. You'd think that having kids is all hunky dory and awesome and smiley, like unicorns flying over rainbows. Wait, unicorns don't fly. Fine, unicorns with wings. But I digress.

So this is why I wrote this book. To let parents everywhere know that they are not alone. That parenting is hard for everyone. Being preggers, breastfeeding, tantrums, explosive blowout diapers, bedtimes, naptimes, scraping projectile vomit off the ceiling, scraping projectile poop off the wall, the terrible twos, the terrible threes, the terrible fours, etc etc etc.

Okay, pardon me while I get all serious for a moment here. Picture a mom who just had a baby for the first time. Her hormones are bouncing off the walls like a pinball machine that's being played by a kid who just chugged four Red Bulls, her nipples feel like they're being eaten by fire ants, and her new baby hasn't let her sleep more than two straight hours in the past three weeks. This little tiny being is constantly with her, and yet she's never felt so alone. This is the reason I wrote this book.

Picture a mom standing in the middle of a supermarket where her kid is literally going cuckoo for Cocoa Puffs because she won't buy them, and everyone in the store is staring at her like she is the worst parent on earth. This is the reason I wrote this book.

Picture a mom looking at the clock figuring out that she has exactly 84 minutes until her husband comes home from work. Or a dad knowing he has exactly 176 days until his wife comes home from Afghanistan. Or a mom doing it all alone day after day because she's single. This is the reason I wrote this book.

Kids are awesome. We love them to death and once we have them we can't imagine life without them. But they're also little a-holes who torture us on a daily basis and make us feel like we're doing it all wrong. This is the reason I wrote this book. To make people laugh and feel a little less alone in the impossible, awesome, horrendous, amazing, challenging, exciting, disgusting, unbelievable job of being a parent.

SHORT IS THE NEW LONG

The days of bios that rival the length of your book are gone. Keep it short because, while people do care who wrote the book, they don't care enough to read paragraphs upon paragraphs about you. Save the long one for your website, the foundation of your infrastructure, and where readers will go when they want to learn even more about you!

INCLUDE A CALL TO ACTION & HOW READERS CAN FIND YOU

Do you want your readers to take any action besides buying your book? Are you giving something away on your website? Do you want readers to join your exclusive reader group or your newsletter? Then mention it in your bio. |Don't forget to add your website address so they can find you.

CUSTOMIZE IT & CHANGE IT UP

Your life isn't static, and your bio shouldn't be either ! Is there something going on in the world that ties into your book? Mention it! You should also modify your bio when you win awards, get more mentions, or get some fab new reviews. For example, *"The New York Times calls this book 'groundbreaking…'"* is a review quote you could easily add at the end of your bio for a strong finish. An upcoming release or mention of your other work is also another great reason to tweak it a bit.

Find reasons to change up your bio! You can do it as often as you want, and don't forget the algorithms notice and respond when a book page is updated.

If you're reading this and you're with a traditional publisher, you may be thinking, "They won't let me change my bio!" Trust me, you don't need your publisher to make changes. Just do it on your Amazon Author Central dashboard and—voilà—done and done.

Your bio should be a fluid extension of your author brand, so include a reminder to check it out and see what you can regularly update as part of your monthly book marketing plan. This may seem like a lot, but it serves another purpose: it gets your eyes on your entire book page, and once you're there, you will hopefully be inspired to cast a critical eye on other areas and make updates that could help drive more sales.

AMAZON EBOOK PRICING TIPS

Book pricing is another way you can activate the Amazon system to boost your ranking.

It's important to understand the Amazon royalty system. When you publish through KDP, you can choose either a 35% or a 70% royalty. Initially you might say 70% is a no-brainer. But there's more involved in the decision than you might think.

Amazon has a "sweet spot" when it comes to pricing. The highest-rated eBooks are generally priced between $2.99 and $5.99. This doesn't mean you won't see higher-priced books in top categories, but they typically will bounce up there for a short period of time and then vanish. Consistent sales require better, smarter pricing, especially for first-time authors.

Many authors price books based on word count. While there's some merit to this, keep in mind that if you price your eBook over $10.00, you could be pricing yourself out of the market, especially if you're an indie.

There's another element to eBook pricing, and that's changing the price point of your book on a semi-regular basis. You could have a $1.99 sale, or you could make it free for an eBook promotion. You could also drop the price of the book for a week during launch time to help boost your algorithm results.

My point is, your price doesn't have to remain static. You could reduce it when you run specials, promote new books, and more. This doesn't mean you should change the price of your book daily, or even weekly. But if you have more than one book, you could certainly have at least one of them on sale all the time.

Generally, if an author has three or more titles, I recommend they rotate them in terms of pricing. I suggest this because it helps your Amazon algorithm. Changing the price of one book a month isn't frequent enough, and you'll end up training your potential buyers to simply wait for the lower price. However, keeping your books at one stagnant price is never a good idea if you want to increase your market/reader numbers.

HOW TO BOOST YOUR ORGANIC OPTIMIZATION WITH AMAZON'S PRE-ORDER

One of the newer features on Amazon that I was most excited about when rewriting this book is the algorithm boost you get from a properly done pre-order campaign. As many of you probably already know, Amazon now allows eBook pre-orders for KDP authors, which essentially levels the playing field between traditionally published authors and those who self-publish through KDP. I'll take you through the steps to get your book into pre-order, but first let's look at when and how this may benefit you.

On Amazon's Kindle Pre-Order information page, they say that pre-orders are great for building buzz. True.

But there is a caveat. If you're a new author with no reader base (yet), you really have to power through your pre-order and work it harder than you would if you had a series of books already out there. The key to any pre-order used to be that you really wanted to boost sales to hit a bestseller list right out of the gate, and while for some that's certainly a consideration, the majority of authors should consider other goals.

Sure, bestseller status would be great, but an organic algorithm boost right out of the gate would be even better.

NEWLY PUBLISHED

If you're a newly published author, the idea of a pre-order seems super-enticing, right? Your book is up on the Amazon site while you count down the days towards its release.

It is pretty exciting, but spend your marketing time wisely. Don't spend a ton of time marketing your pre-order page at this point, because even if you have a fan base you likely won't get a ton of orders.

Sure, you can do a small push to friends and family and to a mailing list if you have one, but at this point it's smarter to start playing with Amazon ads, categories and keyword strings to help the Amazon algorithm kick in.

Your work should be divided into the pieces that help kick-start the algorithm on Amazon (which will benefit you long-term) and the work you can do after the book launches. We'll look at a specific pre-order plan later on in the book.

ALREADY PUBLISHED

If you have a book out there (or several), and you've built a mailing list of fans, then pre-order can build excitement for your upcoming book. But most, if not all, of your marketing should be reserved for when the book is available on Amazon, because that will result in a much bigger benefit for you.

Unless you are JK Rowling or some other mega-bestseller, it's not easy to drive significant numbers to your pre-order page. The other issue you run into is if a reader wants something now, they may not want to wait for your book to be ready and could end up buying something else instead. That said, pre-order can be a lot of fun for fans who've been waiting for your next book.

But even in the case of an established author, your pre-order time should be focused on giving an algorithm kick to your Amazon book page, which will benefit you in the long term.

LONG VERSUS SHORT

Regardless of the category you're in, don't stretch the pre-order time to the full 90 days Amazon allows. If you aren't spending a ton of time promoting the book, you don't want it up for too long. I'd recommend a month, maybe even less—my ideal would be actually two weeks. But those two weeks should be spent on a solid, focused effort which we'll walk through shortly.

Don't fail to hit the deadline you assigned to the pre-order, because once you select it, as we'll see shortly, you can't go back! Pick a date you *know* you can hit. As of this printing, Amazon penalizes authors who miss their pre-order date.

THE AMAZON ALGORITHM FOR PRE-ORDERS

As I've said earlier in this book, when it comes to Amazon, everything matters. This includes your pre-order.

I discovered this with the last edition of this book which I put up for pre-order for two weeks. During that time, I started pushing Amazon ads as soon as the book page went live, and this early ad run helped push the book up the bestseller list. We also did a promotion, which we'll talk about in the next section.

The bottom line is, there's a certain amount of momentum that a book captures organically when it launches on Amazon. It sits in the "new release" section of Amazon, which can be a great spot to attract additional interest.

However, be advised that if your book is on pre-order and then hits the Amazon system on launch day with little to no buzz, no reviews, and no activity, it'll quickly plummet (due to low sales) which is really hard to recover from.

Books that sink down the Amazon list on launch day can take a long time to resurrect. In the testing I've done, I've seen this kind of recovery sometimes take three months or longer. But even if you have no immediate reviews, running ads will help keep the book spiking within its category.

In order to avoid your book tanking on Amazon, you do need to plan a solid promotional campaign for the day it launches—and again, we'll cover this later on in the book!

PROMOTION

You can start to drive some interest to the book by letting your friends, family, and followers know it's coming. However, be warned that your relationship with your followers needs to be about more than just pushing your book—that will get old fast and could lose you buyers.

You can also use your cover or other images in social media posts, blog posts, Amazon ads and so on to promote your book, and in a moment

I'm going to tell you about our most recent successful promotion. When we get to the chapters about promotions later on, we'll dig into some more things you can do to help boost your pre-order sales.

When the prior edition of this book launched, we decided to do a new kind of promotion. It was essentially a buy one, get one—but instead of gifting a second book, we gave readers who pre-ordered the Amazon book access to our Master Amazon Video Program. You may be reading this book because you were part of that promotion.

It went so well that we'll no doubt repeat it for the 2021 edition. The push for pre-orders within a short window really helped the book build up a strong head of steam before the actual launch day, when it just exploded. In fact, if you've taken one of my classes recently, you know I lead off with all the bestseller status ribbons this book has earned.

Sometimes these flags last days or months, other times they last just hours. But regardless of how long you get a bestseller flag, if you've ever had one you know how incredible it feels, right?

In previous editions of the book we've given away second copies of the book—so you buy one and gift one to a friend. That's gone over well, and it's certainly a great strategy, but if you have anything else to give readers access to, that might generate an even stronger motivation for them to preorder, then do so! You could give them one of your other books for free if they buy your current one, or if the book is part of a series you could gift them an earlier book in the series if they haven't read it. Some authors give tote bags. But regardless of the "gift," make it as creative and original as you can.

Whether this is your first or tenth book, to promote your pre-order properly, you'll need to do more than just buzz it to your followers and your e-mail list. Again, if this is your second, third, or fourth book, interest is going to be stronger than with your first.

Remember, offering some kind of a promotional bonus will always help boost sales!

REVIEWS

Keep in mind that readers can't review a pre-order book. If you're looking to get some early reviews, consider focusing on Goodreads, where you can push for pre-order reviews and provide what are called ARCs (advance reader copies) to potential reviewers. You could also do an early giveaway, which we'll discuss in the Goodreads chapter.

PRICING YOUR PRE-ORDER

As mentioned earlier, there's a sweet spot in pricing. I would keep it low, even if you plan to raise the price later. You're competing with millions of titles on Amazon, and your book isn't even out yet. If you want to entice an impulse buy, keep the pricing low at first. Once the book is live, you can always raise the price.

HOW TO SET UP YOUR PRE-ORDER

First and foremost, you need to be a KDP author. Your eBook should be uploaded into the KDP system via their author/book dashboard. Once you're there, you'll see this:

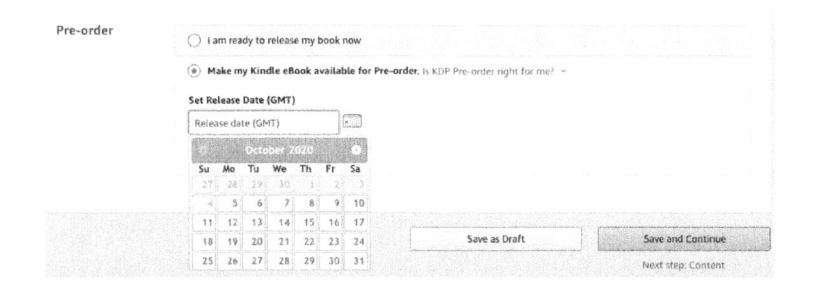

Once you select a date, the system will tell you that you must get the final book to Amazon no later than four days prior. Additionally, you will need to upload a manuscript for them to approve before they'll set up your pre-order. The manuscript doesn't have to be pre-edited; they just want to see what you plan to publish. You'll need a cover, but it doesn't have to be a final version. If you're still a month out with no cover (it happens more often than you think), you can leave the cover blank or put up a placeholder, then add your cover before the pre-order goes live. Here's what the page looks like when it's launched on their site:

According to Amazon, the book can be any length, so if you've written a novella, you can use pre-order too. Currently there are no limitations, other than that you need to be a KDP author, *and, if you're an indie author, this is for eBooks only*.

Pre-order is a fun, cool option for self-published authors, but be mindful of how much of your money and promotional sweat equity you spend. Most readers prefer to buy a book they can read right away. The urge for instant gratification is especially true for eBook readers, because for them, it truly is instant.

THE PERIL OF AMAZON'S ALSO-BOUGHTS

Book marketing is already tough enough without having to wrestle your Amazon book page into submission, too. With Amazon book pages getting increasingly cluttered, it's become harder to find your book amongst the clutter of ads, sidebar stuff, and everything else Amazon is trying to push.

Most of you who read the Author Marketing Experts blog regularly probably know what a book marketing pet peeve this is for me. In fact, I'm kind of a fanatic about keeping that book page clean and user-friendly. This "look" includes your also-boughts—that ribbon of books sandwiched somewhere between your book description, the sponsored posts, and whatever else Amazon is trying to sell to your reader.

Also-bought lists are populated by user preferences. Let's take a reader who normally buys romantic suspense books, lands on your book, reads through the description, maybe reads a few reviews, but then realizes this isn't the book for them. It happens, right? Sure, not every reader who lands on your Amazon book page buys your book (oh, but don't we wish they would?). Let's say the reader in question normally buys books on car mechanics, or poetry or something completely different from what you've written.

Guess what happens? It changes your also-boughts. Because even though the name implies "bought" it's not always the case that the reader has to actually buy your book, because sometimes this algorithm is based on simply landing on your page. I've tested this with my own books, inviting folks who don't normally buy books on book marketing to just land on the page without making a purchase. Guess what happened? My also-boughts changed!

It happens a lot. Authors publish a book and very excitedly, shoot out a note to all their friends to buy a copy. Some will, and some won't, but it's likely that they will visit the book page (if just out of curiosity). Now, if all of your friends buy books in your genre, you're fine, but if Aunt Bethany normally buys books on quilting and you've just published your new sci-fi thriller—guess what? Quilting books will start to populate in your also-bought section.

Why does this matter? Because when it comes to Amazon, everything matters.

E-V-E-R-Y-T-H-I-N-G matters.

Don't ignore your also-boughts! Let's have a look at some reasons, both organic and visual, why this all matters to your book sales.

MESSES WITH YOUR ALGORITHM

It's hard to prove the Amazon algorithm, meaning that, an invisible force is at work behind the scenes, so it's increasingly more challenging to figure out what tips it in your favor and what does not. What I know from books I've tested is that having a messed-up list of also-boughts does impact your visibility on Amazon. It makes sense, right? There isn't an actual person shelving the also-boughts on your page, it's a machine—and machine learning can be tricky.

Machines learn what you show them, and if what you show them is quilting books belong with sci-fi, that's how your book will start showing up, and that's where Amazon will think your book belongs. See the problem? This could impact anything you're doing on Amazon, from running Amazon ads, to discounted eBook promotions—everything. In a minute, I'll cover what to do and how to fix this if it's happening to you.

MAY MISRANK YOUR BOOK(S)

Not that dissimilar from messing with your algorithm, the also-boughts can also misrank your books. You will notice this when you look at the "book details" and see it listed in some odd category. Book details, if you aren't familiar with where to find these, are around the middle of your book page. Included in the book details are things like page count, year published, etc.

INTERRUPTS THE USER EXPERIENCE

When I teach classes on website SEO, ranking, and how to attract more people to your website (and keep them there), one thing I talk about is the user experience. You want to keep everything on your website in line with user expectations. This means if you're selling books about car mechanics, don't pop up a picture of your new puppy, because that's not why people landed on your website.

The same is true for your Amazon book page. As I mentioned earlier, I'm a fanatic about a good user experience, and part of that is your also-boughts. Interrupting the user experience by showing books on quilting on your sci-fi book page could lose browsers—because it takes less than a second to lose a browser to your site. This may not seem like a big thing to you, but in the world of web design and user experience, it's huge. Your Amazon book page is an extension of your website and, as I mentioned before—everything matters.

PREVENTING AN ALSO-BOUGHT MIX-UP

This part is both easy and not easy. First off, the first days your book is live on Amazon are the most critical. Because Amazon is still "learning" about your book, you have no history with Amazon for that particular title, so machine learning is busy trying to dig in and understand your title.

As hard as it may seem, I encourage you to not invite all your family and friends to your book page, at least not right away. Wait till the also-boughts have started populating (this could take a few weeks). I know it's hard. You just published a book, you want to share it with the world, I get it. But trust me, it's a lot harder to clean a potential mess up later.

Alternatively, if your family and friends are a bit internet savvy, you could invite them to visit your book from an incognito page, which won't pull in any potential buyer preferences, although they won't be able to buy your book that way.

A better option would be to invite them to your website, where you can sell your book *and* autograph it for them. Yes, you'll have to mail the books—but you'll also get to personalize them. People (especially friends and family) will love this special touch, and if you're near a holiday (and even if you're not) offer a BOGO—if someone buys your book from your website, offer to send an eBook to a friend of their choosing.

RESOLVING MESSED UP ALSO-BOUGHTS

If you're reading this and and are saying, "Yep, I have a bunch of quilting books on my sci-fi book page." You may be thinking it's already too late for you, and you may be wondering what you can do about it.

Two things: First, you can start to promote the heck out of your book to the right market. Although in some cases, it can take 90 days for also-boughts to fix themselves.

Second, running Amazon ads may help, because if your keywords are spot-on, you're pulling exactly the right reader to your book, which could help speed up the process. A messed-up list of also-boughts doesn't last forever, though. It will eventually right itself, but it will take time.

When it comes to Amazon, keeping an eye on that ever-important book page is a critical component of your success. Whether it's the also-boughts, your book description, or the million other fun things you can do with that page—remember: it all matters.

FINDING GREAT KEYWORD STRINGS FOR YOUR AMAZON ADS

If you're doing a keyword-based ad, it goes without saying that the key words should matter. Of all the things you do related to setting up your ads, this will take you the most time. The good news is, once you find some good keyword strings, you can probably keep running them for as long as you want to run your ads.

Amazon caps your keyword strings at 1,000—though to start with, I'd recommend looking for 300 to 400 keywords/keyword strings. I know this seems like a lot, but there are some easy ways and fun shortcuts for collecting them that I'll share with you later.

Finding keyword strings isn't as hard as you might think. If you've gotten this far in the book and read the chapters about Amazon keyword strings, you know I like to talk a lot about supply and demand and specifically, high demand, low supply.

One of the biggest problems authors face when choosing keyword strings for their book page, or their Amazon ads, is when they choose words that have very little search momentum or, conversely, are far too competitive. Like "contemporary romance" for a romance novel.

The other thing to consider is the *how*, as in how your consumer searches, and, as we've discussed, consumers search based on their needs. If you have a book about gluten intolerance, your consumer may search for "wheat allergies," because they're coming at this from their pain points, not yours. For the purposes of breaking this down in a way that's easy to implement, I'm going to break down this chapter by keyword strings for fiction vs. keyword strings for nonfiction.

UNDERSTANDING THE DIFFERENT KEYWORD MATCH TYPES

Last year Amazon started expanding what it offers in terms of match types for keywords. Currently, they offer broad, phrase, and exact keyword matches. Let's look at what this means and why it matters.

Match types will pull in different audiences, so it's important to understand the distinction before you jump into the process of adding your keyword strings. There is a shortcut around this, as I'll soon show you.

FOR NOW, LET'S SEE WHAT EACH OF THEM MEANS:

Broad Match Search: This is the most flexible of keyword match types, allowing your keyword to show up in a variety of forms. For example, let's say your keyword is Star Wars. Your ad could show up for searches including: Star Wars Movie, Star Wars Book, or Star Wars T-shirt. Conversely, it could also show up for movie Star Wars, book Star Wars, and so on. Broad gives you a lot of flexibility, but it's also a bit like casting a very wide net, which may work in some instances, but it could also start adding up in terms of paying for clicks on keyword terms that aren't related to you at all. An example of this would be using "Star Wars T-shirt" if all you have to offer is a book.

Phrase Match Search: This is a bit less flexible, but also broad enough to pull in a good number of searches. Phrase match allows you to narrow your search terms using specific phrases. The key feature with this particular match type is that it allows you to control the word order. This helps to eliminate searches where a reader inserts a word (like the term "used") in between your keyword strings. However, it will include words before or after your keyword phrase. While it's similar to broad match, it still keeps it within your target market. If you have keyword strings like "Star Wars book," it won't show for T-shirts, mouse pads, or any other Star Wars paraphernalia.

Exact Match Search: This is the most limited of all search terms, and while this may seem like a bad thing, there are phrases that certainly can work well within the parameters of specific words. You should know that using exact match will limit your options, and that's okay if it's what you're trying to accomplish. For example, using Star Wars books will bring up searches for Star Wars book, but not book Star Wars.

WHICH MATCH TYPE IS RIGHT FOR YOUR AD CAMPAIGN?

The short answer is: try them all.

The long answer is a bit more involved and, frankly, in nearly all of the ads that I run, I will often add the keyword strings and experiment with different match types. I'll add each set of keyword strings and then isolate each by Phrase, Exact, and Broad match. That way I can see which keyword strings do better in terms of each match type. This approach is one of the biggest shortcuts to finding keywords: find 100-200 and then rate them under each match type, because you never know what'll stick.

In some cases, like author names, you may not want to use broad match, because if the author has too much "other" stuff, like a non-book product, you could wind up in too many non-relevant searches. But you can start with saving these names using all the matches and see which search term makes you money versus which one costs you money.

AUTHOR NAMES AND BOOK TITLES AS KEYWORD STRINGS

This is still a recommended strategy, though I tend to use it more often for fiction than nonfiction. As you experiment with this, you may find that the broad match isn't best match type for names, but this does vary. This concept will appear later in the section on ad reports .

AMAZON'S KEYWORD SUGGESTIONS

Initially Amazon's suggestions are bad, but at some point (7-10 days post launch) they will start improving and continue to get better from there. When you're adding keywords into your dashboard, you'll see Amazon's autocomplete pop up. Pay close attention, because it could offer some insights into the keywords you will want to use in addition to what you already have used. Keyword suggestions and autocomplete are two different animals, and I'm not sure why one is less accurate than the other, but I've played with the autocomplete and I really like some of the keywords I'm being offered!

NEGATIVE KEYWORD STRINGS

Using negative keyword strings in the right way is another great opportunity to narrow your searches and to avoid spending money on ads that aren't working for you. Keyword strings you want to rank as negative should be used carefully, because you don't want to omit searches that could be great for your sales.

But you should consider various subgenres if you're writing genre fiction in particular.

Romance readers are pretty specific in what they're looking for. Christian romance readers don't want to be shown a bunch of erotic romance. Therefore, you may want to include "Christian romance" or "sweet romance" as negative keywords so you aren't wasting money turning up in those searches. Conversely, if you have a sweet romance, you probably don't want to show up under an erotic or steamy romance search.

Science fiction also has a lot of micro-genres that you'll want to be sensitive to, so it's helpful if you're hyper-focused on any nuances or subgenre you know your book won't appeal to.

Even nonfiction falls under this, depending on the book topic. Your book may appeal to a specific niche, like a beginning investor, so adding the words like "seasoned investor" to your negative keywords dashboard might be a good thing.

At a minimum, I recommend also including the term "used" in your negative keywords list (unless you're selling used books), and keeping an eye on your dashboard to see what's pulling in traffic and what's wasting money. You can always add to your negative keyword dashboard, too. You could also add the word "free" to your negative keywords so you aren't coming up if readers are searching for free eBooks.

FINDING YOUR KEYWORD STRINGS

In the following section I'm going to divide up the search protocols by fiction and nonfiction, because these two keyword searches are vastly different from what they used to be. First, we'll look at finding nonfiction keyword strings to match your sales objectives.

KEYWORD STRINGS FOR NONFICTION

Amazon's new ad system radically changed how we search for nonfiction keyword strings, and it's become much more aligned with Google searches, so that in large part, you can use Google to find your keyword strings.

If you've ever run a Google ad campaign, you're probably already familiar with their Keyword Planner tool, but if you're not, it's very easy to use. You could also use any keyword planner tool you have access to, even Ubersuggest, which is free. We use it a lot to define keywords for our website, so it's a great way to start digging through keywords to find the ones that will most resonate with your readers.

One thing I like to do when I'm searching for keyword strings for Amazon is dig into the needs of the readers searching. Earlier in this book I described finding keyword strings for an Amazon optimization I did for a book on breathing better and earlier I discussed how *the reader is searching for the problem*, not the issue itself.

The same is true for your ads. Though "breathing better" will most definitely be part of your keyword strings, you'll also want to add the reader "pain points" to your list, which means you need to learn what's bringing them to your book. If you don't know this, you can play around with your preferred keyword tool, or just start doing a search on Amazon and see what pops up. You'll quickly discover what's being purchased and what isn't.

Unlike what's been recommended in previous editions of this book, your ad keywords research will need to very closely match your book keywords, in the sense that you'll want to find keyword strings and books that have a good sales rank. By "good" I mean 50,000 or less.

Let's have a look at one keyword string: saving money for retirement. This one follows what I've talked about previously: supply and demand.

Very little supply and the sales rank of the books shows a reasonably high demand:

```
1-16 of 951 results for Kindle Store : "saving money for retirement"                    Sort by: Featured
```

Check out the sales rank for the eBook:

Product details
File Size : 4761 KB
Publication Date : December 10, 2008
Word Wise : Enabled
Print Length : 366 pages
Publisher : Penguin Books; Revised Edition (December 10, 2008)
Language: : English
ASIN : B0052MD8VO
X-Ray : Enabled
Text-to-Speech : Enabled
Enhanced Typesetting : Enabled
Lending : Not Enabled
Best Sellers Rank: #6,727 in Kindle Store (See Top 100 in Kindle Store)
   #6 in Personal Money Management (Kindle Store)
   #23 in Personal Success in Business
   #33 in Budgeting & Money Management (Books)
Customer Reviews: ★★★★☆ · 1,310 ratings

Related video shorts (0) Upload your video

And now the sales rank for the print book:

Product details
Item Weight : 9.6 ounces
Paperback : 368 pages
ISBN-10 : 9780143115762
ISBN-13 : 978-0143115762
Product Dimensions : 0.8 x 5 x 7.6 inches
Publisher : Penguin Books; Revised Edition (December 10, 2008)
Language: : English
ASIN : 0143115766
Best Sellers Rank: #3,811 in Books (See Top 100 in Books)
   #25 in Budgeting & Money Management (Books)
   #176 in Success Self-Help
Customer Reviews: ★★★★☆ · 1,310 ratings

AMAZON'S KEYWORD SUGGESTIONS FOR NONFICTION

Previous versions of the AMS dashboard have offered an unimpressive list of keyword suggestions, and they still do…and they're still not very impressive. But as your ads age, these keyword suggestions start to improve while Amazon learns your ad. When you're setting up your ad, you certainly want to consider them, but if you check the keyword suggestions again in 7-10 days, you'll see a vast improvement.

USING AUTHOR NAMES AND BOOK TITLES

The previous example "saving for retirement" showed a keyword string I'd absolutely add to my ads dashboard, but it also unearthed books I'd add, too. Your keywords should be a healthy blend of keyword strings, book titles, and author names. How many of each is hard to predict, meaning there isn't an exact metric for 20% of this and 50% of that. The exact blend will depend on how your ad does with each set.

USING ALSO-BOUGHTS

Much like with the optimization chapters, you can absolutely use also-boughts as part of your keyword strings (book titles and authors). Just remember the same rules apply: make sure the sales rank is solid.

KEYWORD STRINGS FOR GENRE FICTION

Genre fiction always seems more successful when you use other author names and book titles, so let's start there. Again, just as I advised in the nonfiction guidance above, you'll want to look for searches that are pulling in lots of traffic, and authors who are selling lots of books. A sales rank of 50,000 and less is great, overall—but obviously even better if it's a lower number than that.

An easy way to get started is to grab authors from your previous also-boughts.

To the right is an example of an author page from one of our AME authors, and you can see under the Also Bought section that there's a pre-populated list to get us started.

Basically, what I'm going to do is start with these authors, using their names and book titles, and start building my keyword strings list. Just click on any author, and it'll pull up their page and list of their books. Then start taking notes!

I may also go to the also-bought list on these authors' pages, too, and keep building until I'm satisfied with the number of keyword strings I have.

Remember, you can use non-author and book title keywords, too—just like you did in your book optimization! In fact, if you've already done that, go ahead and start using some of them in your ads!

> Seasonal keywords are another fun element you can add. For example: *summer romance read, tax time help, beach read, holiday romance.* You can add them during the season and remove them when the season is over!

KEYWORD STRINGS FOR MEMOIRS, LITERARY FICTION, WOMEN'S FICTION

These keyword strings will fall into the same bucket as mentioned above, except you might be more inclined to pull in keyword strings readers are using in their searches. For example, in the case of a memoir about Alzheimer's, you might use the term: Alzheimer's in your keyword, and so on.

CHILDREN'S FICTION, YOUNG ADULT FICTION

Much like the above, your keyword strings for children's and young adult books may be better served by a blend of author titles and solutions. For example, a children's book on kindness might benefit from the keyword string: teaching children kindness.

KILLING OFF KEYWORDS— WHEN TO DO IT AND WHY YOU'D WANT TO

Remember when I talked about Amazon's relevancy score? Well keywords, for obvious reasons, factor heavily into this, so don't hesitate to kill off keywords that are draining your budget. How soon should you kill them off? I'd give them 5–7 days for the ads to gain some traction and start killing them off after that.

> There are keyword experts who like to talk about doubling up keywords—for example, the term "book book book" is really popular on Amazon, because of...well, books. But using that one won't get you a good return on your ads. Instead, consider doubling up on keywords that are performing. For example, if "book marketing" is performing, I'd do a keywork string that reads: book marketing book marketing. It doesn't work in every case, but you can try it and see how the keywords do!

ONE FINAL NOTE ABOUT KEYWORD STRINGS

When you include book titles, I recommend staying away from one-word titles. I haven't personally achieved an affordable CPC (cost per click) by using them. For example: "Hot," or "Smokin'," which you tend to see a lot in romance, are probably too broad and won't get you a good kickback in search. Or worse, it'll cost you a lot of money and yield very little in sales.

I recommend starting with 300-400 keyword strings. However, keep in mind that you can pair these by using the different search matches (broad, phrase, and exact)—thereby decreasing the number of keywords you need to actually search. Also, keep in mind that you can always add to your keywords, and keep adding to them if the ad is doing well!

ADDING KEYWORD STRINGS TO YOUR ADS

The final step is adding your keyword strings to your ad. You'll want to add them manually since uploading an Excel file never seems to work. As you'll see, the Match Types are already checked for you, so when you add your keywords you don't have to re-add them under the various match types, which makes it easy.

PRODUCT TARGETING ADS

Product targeting is exactly what the name says: you're targeting other, similar books in your market. I like this a lot, actually, and there's a chance we may flip all of our authors (especially fiction) into doing only product targeting, and here's why: keywords require a lot more care and feeding.

You have to manage them, make sure the bids are set, lower them if they're too high, and kill them if they aren't working. I don't mean to imply that product targeting doesn't require attention. It does. But it's different, in that you're finding specific books to align with. Yes, you can do that with author names and book titles, absolutely. But if you're ready to get even more granular, product targeting is a great addition to your ad sets.

To get started, you'll want to find books and authors to align with. If you're already running a successful keyword campaign and have your author names and book titles, that's a good place to start. You're going to locate and save the books ASIN numbers or ISBN numbers. Why the difference? Because it's important to understand your readers' buying habits.

UNDERSTAND BUYING HABITS

Regardless of what you're advertising on Amazon, it's important to understand your readers' buying habits. Readers who buy only eBooks won't be persuaded to buy print if it's not what they're accustomed to. By the same token, readers who buy books in print tend to buy more print.

I mention this here because while you're digging for books for your product placement ads, be sure to find ones for the formats your reader prefers. In general, genre fiction tends to be heavily eBook-driven, whereas business books and literary fiction tend to be very print book-focused.

Not sure which format resonates most with your readership? You can start by doing a little Amazon research and comparing sales ranks of print versus eBook on the book page itself. Check out the top titles in your market and see which sales rank seems to be lower.

You can also look at their also-boughts to get a sense of preferred book formats, as well as popular books in your genre or niche.

Buying habits matter, especially with book formats, because by default Amazon will show your book ads regardless of format. For example, it's been my experience that Amazon will show eBook ads on paperback or hardcover books. If your reader is predisposed to paperback, you've now wasted money on your ad. But targeting ASIN numbers (if you want your ads to show in eBooks) will better reach your audience, and your ads will do better.

SETTING UP PRODUCT TARGETING ADS

Since the setup dashboard is the same for keyword or product targeting, you'll just pick "product targeting" under the "targeting" options. When you do, it flips the bidding area to "categories" and "individual products"

```
Product targeting

Default bid
$  0.75

Categories    Individual Products

Suggested    Search

1 suggestion                                                          Target all

/Books/Reference/Writing, Research and Publishing/Book Publishing Reference/Authorship Reference
Authorship Reference                                                  Target   Refine
```

I like adding categories to these ads as well as products, which you can do from the same dashboard by popping in either the author name or specific ASIN numbers. Be aware that if you do a keyword search here it will almost always pull up products, too.

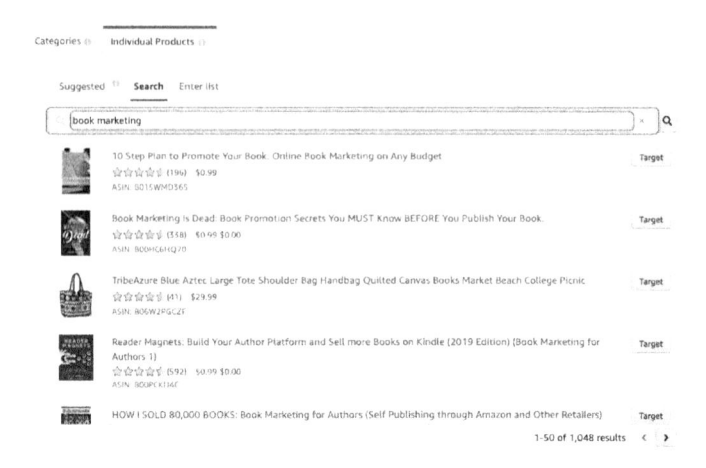

So how many do you need? Consider starting with 25–50 and keep adding from there. You don't need as many to start with as you do with keywords, because keywords have to be managed more carefully, and not all keywords will work, as earlier mentioned.

You may be thinking at this point that product targeting sounds much easier than keywords, and it is. But it doesn't work well for all books.

Mine, for example, do much better with keyword targeting. This is partly because there aren't a ton of books on book marketing—none that are new, anyway. I top out at 20–25 books to target, and in an ideal situation I'd like to start out with more.

But I run this product ad alongside my keyword ads, so it's an enhancement. Especially if you have a limited inventory, you can't run only product targeting; you'll need to do both. If you have a lot of options for books, you could start with product targeting and see how well it does for you.

Remember, the numbers never lie. Watch your CTR, CPC, and ACOS for a true indicator of how your ad set is doing.

A FINAL NOTE ON PRODUCT TARGETING ADS

If your book matches with a product, there's no reason you can't advertise alongside it. For example, if you have a Star Wars-related book, you could advertise alongside the release of the latest Star Wars movie. Or if you have a fun book about kids making Christmas decorations, you could advertise it next to Christmas stuff, or decorating, or whatever. Also, consider running your holiday romance advertising next to a Hallmark movie or something similar!

Consider book pairing, when appropriate, not least because you can have some fun with it as well!

RUNNING ADS INTERNATIONALLY

If you have a book that appeals to an international market, running ads in other countries might be a great sales tool. Currently you can run ads in the UK, Germany, France, Spain, and Italy.

Each dashboard does need to be set up independently; you can't incorporate the dashboard into your US one. You have to log in and out of each of the various countries, which can be a hassle, but it's certainly worth it if you want to reach international markets.

Genre fiction tends to do well in many international markets, so you might want to advertise your thriller in Germany because many people speak English there. If you have a book translated into Spanish or Italian, it's a given that you'd want to advertise on those platforms.

If your book isn't genre fiction or translated, you could still experiment with ads in the UK, which are currently 30% less expensive than running them in the US. Be aware that if you do this, I wouldn't recommend copying your keywords directly over from your US ads, because searches and results will be different on the UK Amazon platform. It'll be best if you do your research from scratch.

The international ads dashboard is quite similar to the US dashboard, except you can't do ad copy at all (At least as of this writing. That might change down the road) and you can't do product targeting (yet), only keyword targeting. Other than that, all of the same rules apply.

I encourage you to have an eBook, if you don't already. Shipping internationally can be a challenge (often cost-prohibitive) and while eBooks aren't as big internationally as they are here, I had no trouble getting ad traction on my UK dashboard with my eBook.

International ads are fun to experiment with and they cost a lot less than the US ads dashboard, so you may want to give them a try.

WRITING A GREAT BOOK AD

If you've ever done Google Ads, Facebook ads, or Twitter, you already know that you don't get a lot of room to work with in terms of ad content, so keep it short and sweet.

Statistics like percentages, and numbers like "top 5," are great attention-grabbers, so if you can find a way to work them in and they make sense for your topic, do it.

I also find it helps to link the ad content to keyword strings you plan to use when at all possible. By linking keyword strings to ads, you're also giving them the best chance to be seen, when you make sure the keyword strings match those in the ad.

For example, I linked an ad with keyword strings like "book marketing," "book promotion," and "book success," and the ad had the same keyword strings in it. Essentially, what happens when you do this is Google sees the ad with all the keyword strings supporting it and gives it more visibility because there's more of a match.

If you are truly stuck for books, authors, and keyword strings, and barely made it to 200 or 300, you may be stuck and unable to do a variety of ads. That's okay, this isn't a deal-breaker. Your ads will still work well enough to make them worth your while.

FURTHER CUSTOMIZING YOUR ADS

However, if you wind up with a ton of keyword strings, or you want to explore more areas, let's take a minute to discuss customizing ads to specific topics, specialties, or areas of focus.

Let's say your book fits in a few areas, which most books do. For example, you might have a book about growing a new business, gluten intolerance, food allergies, or even a genre fiction book. Each of these titles has a subset of interest that you probably found in your book research.

For the small business book, you might have found strings of keywords that talked about the importance of promoting your business on social media, and maybe even found a whole bunch of great social media books. Or maybe there's a chapter or two in your book about business accounting, and you found a whole slew of books about setting up accounting procedures if you're in a new business. Each of these areas of focus likely brought up a number of keyword strings, as well as book titles and authors. I would recommend grouping some of your ads to serve a particular market segment if you have enough keyword strings and a big enough ad budget to do so.

What you'll do next, to use the business book example, is use words like "social media" if you're tying into your string of social media and marketing books. Or "simple accounting" if you're after business owners who need to focus on this. Make sense?

One thing I don't recommend is running ads with book blurbs/reviews. Blurbs are great, but remember you've got a split second to drive interest to your ad, so you want whatever copy you've put in that ad to connect to your reader in an instant. If you've written genre fiction, be mindful of the tropes your reader responds to, and if you've written non-fiction, what is the main benefit your reader is looking for?

> Whatever keywords you're using for your ads, use them whenever possible on your Amazon book page, too. Whether it's in the book description or your author interview, sprinkling them throughout your book page can also help with ad relevancy. What I recommend is watch your ads until you've found the handful of keyword strings that are really helping to push sales and use those!

WRITING YOUR AD

If you're doing ads based on keyword strings, you'll want to include some of the keyword strings in the ad itself. If you aren't, and you aren't sure where to start, do a search on Amazon in your genre, niche, or subject, and see what kinds of Sponsored Posts get your attention. The ads are all pretty short in terms of word count, so you don't have a lot of room to work with anyway.

Something I've also done is create two identical campaigns using the same keyword strings, only with different ads, especially different ad copy, to see which gets the greater number of impressions. Keep in mind that 1,000 impressions mean it was shown to 1,000 customers, and you need around 1,000 impressions to determine how well the ad (and keywords) are working.

RUNNING ADS WITHOUT AD COPY

Amazon now gives you the option to run book ads without ad copy, and if you do this you can promote multiple books in one ad. While I've seen ad copy make a difference, I've also seen cases where it doesn't matter, and this is often where and how your ad is shown—on a search page, vs. on the actual book page. Amazon can sometimes show your ad without ad copy, even if you included when you created the ad. And there's some data to suggest that a reader is more swayed by the number of reviews, book cover, and price than anything else. You may want to try two ad sets, one with copy and one without, and see which does better for you.

AMAZON ADS: REPORTS

Reporting is important and, thankfully, Amazon provides you with a lot of tools.

First, let's look at the side panel of each ad set and uncover what each of the tabs offer. If you're running an ad, you can see on the left that you have a few options to help you dig into your ads even more deeply.

I'll give you a rundown of the most important ones to look at. Mind you, they're all important in terms of mining data, but some will matter more than others:

- **Placements:** This tab will show you where your ads are being seen, and how much they're being engaged with in the places where your ads are being shown. This is a very good indicator of how well your ad copy is working, too, plus it's a great indicator of whether you need ad copy or not. Remember we talked about where some ads show up versus where other ads are showing?

    Ads that show top of search (on the search page, not the book page)—show up without ad copy. But copy does show up on the actual book page.

    When I reviewed my placements, found that my CTR was much higher for top-of-page, which makes sense, given the placement. When the ad is on the book page, the competition is much greater. The ad still does well, but the CTR is lower, again because of the competition. Across the board, I've seen books do better in top-of-search, it'll cost you more, but if you want to change the bid to hit that mark, you can do it from the dashboard above.

- **Search Terms:** This is another fun one, especially if you're doing a keyword-based ad. This will show you what keywords your ads are being triggered from. I check this one a lot, actually, both because I may want to add keywords from this list, ones I hadn't considered. Or I can remove keywords that are triggering a lot of clicks and no buys.

- **Campaign Settings:** As the name implies, you can modify ad settings here.

- **History:** I don't use this one much. I like the actual reporting feature better.

AMAZON REPORTS

If you're running multiple ads, Amazon reports are really great because you can see, in one place, how the ads are doing without having to click in and out of dashboards. I run them once a month.

The report has so many columns, it may seem overwhelming at first. If you're familiar with Excel, you already know you can easily right click on a column and hide it. But you can also sort the reports by a variety of columns. I love looking at the CTR vs. impressions, customer search term and RoAS (Return on Ad Spend).

I will often sort these reports by CTR (column K) to see what keywords are getting the most clicks. I'll also look at the Customer Search Term column too, because that often shows keywords I may have missed, or ones I might want to add to the negative search terms if they aren't converting.

Column J shows you which search terms got the most clicks, which means you'll get a good sense of what your most profitable keywords are and, if you're running multiple ads, you may want to add them to other ad sets if you haven't already done so.

Column H is "Customer Search Term," which I've mentioned a few times. It provides good insights into keywords you may want to add, but it could also show you products you might want to target too, if the search terms are showing book titles. It's a good one to watch as well.

Another report you can run is a keyword analysis. You can do this by selecting "targeting" in the dropdown under the report menu:

```
Configuration

    Campaign type    ● Sponsored Products
                     ○ Sponsored Brands
      Report type
        Time unit    Search term
                     Targeting
                     Advertised product
    Report period    Campaign
                     Placement
                     Performance Over Time
```

When you select "targeting," it will show you in even more detail which keyword strings were targeted with your ads, and this allows you to determine which keywords to add and which to get rid of.

You can't go wrong with these reports, really. They system auto-runs them in a 14-day window, meaning they cover the past 14 days, and they're a super-helpful way to study and compare the performance of all your ads in one place.

FUN AMAZON HACKS

AMAZON AUTHOR CENTRAL

Every Amazon author, no matter when or what they've published, has an author page which shows up along with your books when you search for the author name on Amazon—*if you've claimed your pages.*

Surprisingly, many authors haven't claimed their pages. If you're not sure whether you've claimed yours yet, head on over to https://authorcentral.amazon.com/. You can access it using your Amazon sign-in. Keep in mind that even if you're traditionally published, you can still have an Amazon author page.

In order to claim the page, you must sign in and add content to the page. Make sure all your books are claimed under your author page. It's easy enough—simply list them in Author Central by inserting their ISBNs or ASINs and posting them to your page. Amazon will double-check your entries for accuracy. Once they do, you'll find a library of your books on your Author Central page.

In addition to your Amazon US page, you should also check out your international pages, which I'll cover in a minute!

Take a look at this standard Amazon author page:

As you can see, this author has added her bio, listed her books, and has book detail pages, which we'll discuss shortly. This works for both print and eBooks—basically, any book you have on Amazon can be added to your Amazon author page via Author Central. Also, notice you can program your author page to show your recent blog posts. There's also an option for your readers to follow your author page, which means they'll get an email from Amazon every time you publish a new book.

FARMING DATA FROM AMAZON AUTHOR CENTRAL

One of the bigger benefits of accessing your Author Central page is the data. An author can now access lots of data about their pages, like sales numbers—both Nielsen BookScan and Amazon data.

If you aren't familiar with Nielsen BookScan, it's the gold standard by which all your print sales are judged. Unlike Amazon sales numbers, which aren't made public, anyone with a BookScan account can access your print sales data. You can also see all your reviews across all your books.

Across the top bar of your Author Central you'll see "sales info" that takes you to the sales data, and this information is invaluable. Keep in mind that the data on this dashboard only refers to Amazon sales. If your publisher has a subscription to Nielsen BookScan independently, they can view data across all sales channels, including bookstores, Target, and Walmart, if the book is being sold there. The Amazon sales data is strictly for their site.

You can also check your author rank, which may also show up on some book pages. Unlike BookScan data, your Author Rank takes into consideration your eBook *and* print sales, across all of Amazon, and also within your genre, so Amazon will let you scroll down and see the breakdown specific to your market.

ADDING REVIEWS TO YOUR BOOK PAGE VIA AUTHOR CENTRAL

Dressing up your Amazon book page is a high priority for authors. Previously we were at the mercy of whoever reviewed the book on Amazon and whatever details the publisher decided to add.

Not anymore. Now you can go in and add reviews *you* choose to help dress up the page.

Here's how: Once your books are listed on your author page after you've connected them to your account—just click on the book title, and it will open to a page that lets you fill in all the back-end detail like your author interview, reviews, etc. It's that easy. You can do the same with endorsements.

The editing possibilities in Amazon are pretty sophisticated, so be sure to bold and italicize portions of your reviews, like headlines and names, whenever possible.

Amazon's editing tools works like Word's, making it easy to draw a potential reader's attention to a particular sentence or section of a review. If you want to know more about how to dress it up, just go back to the chapter How Great Amazon Book Descriptions Help Indie Authors Sell More Books, which gives you step-by-step instructions.

MONITORING REVIEWS ON AMAZON

You can monitor your reviews on Amazon from your Author Central page.

A word to the wise: Thank people for their reviews. It's a great way to spread the love and network with readers and reviewers. But remember, this isn't the place to enter into detailed discussion. A simple thank-you is your best bet. We'll cover more about reviews later.

FOLLOW AUTHOR FEATURE

Encourage your readers to follow you. When they do, they'll automatically be notified whenever you publish a new book or set up a pre-order.

Simply send readers to your page, where they'll find the yellow "Follow" bar under your author photo.

+ Follow

Follow to get new release updates and improved recommendations

ENHANCING YOUR AMAZON HEADLINE

In addition to farming data, adding reviews and monitoring them, and using the "follow" feature, you can add some style-enhancers to your headline when you upload your book through the Amazon dashboard. Although this won't affect your algorithm per se, it will help make your book description more visually appealing.

You can add them via your Author Central page, but if you're uploading the book via KDP, you'll need this code:

Here are some of the headline enhancers available:

- Bolding: The text you want bolded
- Italics: <i>The text you want italicized</i>
- Headline: <h1>The text you want for a headline</h1>

You can add numbered lists and bullet points, too.

ANOTHER BOOST FOR YOUR BOOKS

Within the Author Central dashboard is a very underused, little-known area that can truly help enhance your books. This area includes sections for "From the Author" and "From the Inside Flap," and more. I think it is overlooked a lot because authors don't realize they can get creative.

The space can be used for more than just reviews. You can use it to add a lot of fun, informative enhancements to your Author Central page. Let's look at where to find the page. When you're in your Author Central dashboard, click on Books.

Once you click on a particular book, you'll see this under Editorial Reviews:

Now you can add all sorts of fun stuff to this page. What kinds of things can you add? You can develop your "dream" Q&A as a great way to share all the information you wish the media or readers would ask, or as a smart way to work in a bunch of information that just couldn't fit into your book description.

A personal note from the author is a clever way to drive home why you're passionate about your subject or genre.

Or include information about a contest you're running, or a mention of your social media addresses, website, and more.

I've seen some authors use this space to update their readers about other promotions they're doing, too. For example, when you run discounted promotions or a freebie, mention it here. Amazon says it takes up to 72 hours to update, but I've never had it take that long. Still, plan ahead, because if the Amazon machine gets busy and the update you're making happens in a limited timeframe, you'll want to set it up well ahead of the promo date.

AMAZON VIDEO SHORTS

I love this feature, and it's not just for readers to add their video review of your book. It's also a great tool for authors to use to add enhanced content to your page.

For example, currently we're working with an attorney who was involved with a case against GM a number of years ago. It was a highly publicized case, which was essentially about GM concealing a known deadly issue with their cars, because it was cheaper to let people die and get sued rather than to recall them and correct the defect.

Sounds horrifying doesn't it? In this instance, the attorney (who won the case, by the way) is putting up short clips of his experiences while working on and winning this case. For example: What it was like to go up against a gorilla like GM? What was it like working with parents who had lost children in these accidents, and so on? In one video he talks briefly about the toll this case took on him and his family. I encouraged him to do this series to provide readers with an emotional connection and thus, what they can expect from the book, as well as a personal glimpse of the author.

Video shorts can be used for just about anything. From just a quick "thank you for visiting my Amazon book page" to digging deep and giving readers a sense of where the story came from, why you wrote it, and so on.

THE MOST OVERLOOKED AMAZON SALES TOOL: INTERNATIONAL AUTHOR CENTRAL PAGES!

Have you ever looked at your KDP sales dashboard and wondered how you can sell more books in other countries? We have a client who noticed she's selling a bunch of books in Japan and wondered if she could rack up more sales there.

In addition to pitching specific blogs in those areas, or doing advertising geared to that market, all of which requires time and money, you could also take a few minutes and claim your Author Central pages in those countries. It's quick and easy, and the best part is, all the international Author Central pages are the same.

First, here are the countries that do *not* have Author Central pages set up.

- Brazil
- Canada
- China
- Mexico
- Netherlands

These countries all list your book, but don't have a page connecting all your titles. The irony is most of our authors don't sell a lot of books in these areas unless the book relates to that country specifically. For example, a book about Mexican heritage might do well on Amazon's website in Mexico.

Next, let's look at the countries that do have Author Central pages:

- France
- Japan
- UK
- Germany

A note regarding Japan's Author Central pages: First, you have to register there. Just use the same username and password you use for the US site, and it takes just a few clicks. Don't let the "new registration" deter you.

From there, the system will ask to verify your e-mail, in fact, all the sites do this. Once your e-mail is verified, you're good to go.

YOUR AUTHOR CENTRAL TOOLS

When setting up an International Author Central page, use the Chrome browser. It has a quick "translate" button, which is far more accurate than any others I've tried. It takes one quick step to translate a Japanese website into English. And English to Japanese.

To start, you'll need your bio. You can use whatever bio you created for yourself on your US page, but it might be nice if you adjust it to suit the country you're targeting. For example, let's say you have an international mystery that takes the reader from the UK to Germany and beyond. You might want to address that in your bio, and the international connection could help pull in readers from the countries you mention.

IMAGES AND VIDEO

A while back Amazon removed the ability to "add images" to the actual book page, but it has now returned that ability to the Author Central Page. You can add up to eight images, and the best part is, you can replace them with new images whenever you want. You've released a new book? Add a new image. Or if you have a promotion coming up, or you've won an award, then by all means add an image of the award, too. Readers love learning about your awards!

Your video can be anything from you speaking at an event to an actual book video/trailer. Video is a great enhancement tool. And the best part? You can upload as many as you'd like. I've done as many as three or four.

YOUR BOOKS

The other fun piece about this is that the system is very good at grabbing all your books. Just make sure that you click on the "Books" tab.

amazon Author Central   Author Page   **Books**   Sales Info   Customer Reviews

THE FINAL RESULT!

Here you can check out Author Central Pages across several countries. They're robust, engaging, and keep all the author's books in one place so your readers can easily find them.

- France: https://www.amazon.fr/-/e/B00AB0CHJQ
- Germany: https://www.amazon.de/-/e/B00AB0CHJQ
- Japan: https://www.amazon.co.jp/-/e/B00AB0CHJQ
- UK: https://www.amazon.co.uk/-/e/B00AB0CHJQ

HOW TO ACCESS THESE PAGES

And to make it simple for you, here are the links to access and update each of your pages. Yes, it's that easy!

- France: https://authorcentral.amazon.fr/
- Germany: https://authorcentral.amazon.de/gp/home
- Japan: https://authorcentral.amazon.co.jp/gp/home
- UK: https://authorcentral.amazon.co.uk/gp/home

BUT DOES IT SELL BOOKS?

Yes, I can tell you it does. In fact, authors we've done this for have seen a substantial uptick in international market sales after they updated these pages. Keep in mind that if you're already selling books in these markets, this will help you a great deal. If you aren't selling books in, let's say, Germany, you might not see any immediate effect there. But it's still a fabulous thing to have, update, and optimize!

AMAZON X-RAY

Awhile back Amazon quietly released a new service within its Kindle program called X-Ray. X-Ray is a way to provide additional or enhanced content to your readers via their Kindle devices, and because Amazon doesn't advertise it, most authors and readers overlook it. But if you take the time to play around with it, you'll find it's a pretty fun tool to use.

Here is Amazon's description of what the X-Ray feature is:

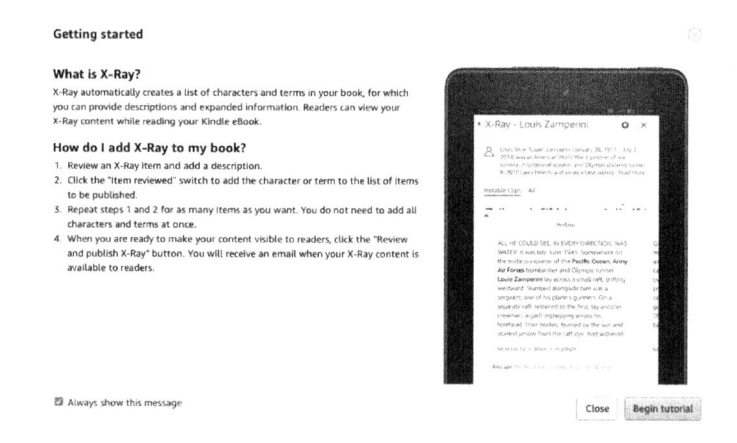

First off, you'll want to get access to the X-Ray feature on your KDP dashboard. If you click the three dots next to your book, it'll pop up as an option:

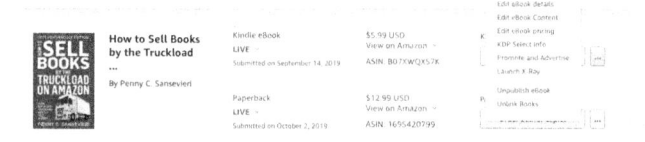

When you click that link, it'll take you to the back-end X-Ray dashboard, where you'll notice that down the left-hand side, most of the character names have the word "published" beside them. This means that content has been published under that character name. If your book is nonfiction, you'll see that, too.

When you access X-Ray, you'll probably see that most of them are already published, and it's because Amazon grabs some random bit of text (as you'll see in the screenshot below) while other times it grabs the Wikipedia description. In my case, they grabbed the description of an actual penny because of my name—which didn't fit the content at all. When you click on the name, it'll open a window like the one below, where you can edit the irrelevant content. The example below is from a fiction book. Leaving the description "Janet was a sure thing" isn't helpful in terms of this feature, and also means something entirely different from what was likely intended.

First and foremost, I suggest that you go through your books and check the X-Ray content. Once you publish it, readers can access it on their Kindle devices or tablets. Which means that they can access the X-Ray link in their tablet by clicking the icon, like this ⟶

They'll be able to see whatever content you added for each character name or keyword. With enhanced content, you'll be able to offer readers more insight into the keyword, the character, or the backstory for whatever it is you're sharing in your book.

It's a fun tool, which can be used not just to add backstory for characters, but to enhance any nonfiction content you may have.

For example, with my own books about book marketing, I went in there and added additional information about particular terms. This works extremely well if you don't want to take readers too far outside of what you're explaining, where enhanced explanations don't necessarily make sense within the text, or if you just want to update the content.

In one of my other marketing books, I had a chapter where I mentioned CreateSpace, which has since been folded into KDP, so I added an enhancement piece and addressed the changes. This was great, because the book wasn't really due for an update, but I could get in there and make some additional changes on X-Ray to give the reader a better, more current experience.

LETTING READERS KNOW ABOUT X-RAY

You may be wondering, since Amazon isn't widely promoting this, why should you care about X-Ray? Well, if you don't care that Amazon may be plugging whatever content they deem necessary into your book, then don't bother with it.

But if you want to be sure your book is the best it can be, and that you have access to and control of your X-Ray content, then I suggest not only getting in there and updating it, but letting readers know to look for it. You could send out a newsletter to your readers, as well as share it on social media. If you plan to do this, you could also mention it in your book intro (this works probably best with nonfiction).

MAKING X-RAY CONTENT FUN

Aside from adding character backstory or enhancing/updating existing nonfiction content, you could also create a sort of Easter egg hunt for fun things you've included in your book that readers can find and perhaps win prizes.

You could also include links to other external content, as well, like blog posts you'd like readers to see, and so on. The links aren't live, so I'd also create a fun, shorter link using a Bit.ly or some other shortening URL service. Bit.ly allows you to customize the link, which makes it easy for a reader to remember or jot down!

CREATIVE WAYS TO BOOST YOUR KEYWORD STRINGS

I've spent quite a bit of time in this book discussing keyword strings, both how to find them and how to use them. I have talked about keyword strings in your book description and subtitle, or even using keyword strings in your title.

But what happens if not all these pieces are an option? Will your book tank? Is there anything else you can do?

Fortunately, the answer is: no, it won't tank your book. However, having more keyword strings on your book page will help it considerably. What can you do? How about an author interview?

This simple tool—a quick, interesting interview with you, the fabulous author, available on your Author Page via Author Central—is a great way to enhance your keyword usage and include more words you might not have been able to add otherwise.

My suggestion for the interview is to keep it interesting enough that readers will want to read the book, because if you're just adding content to be able to shove in more keyword strings, it won't necessarily help holding readers' attention.

Ask a few questions—maybe up to five—and then answer them in such a way that you can use some of your keyword strings. You can also add keyword strings to the questions themselves. Take a look at the following interview done by one of our authors:

GET TO KNOW CHRISTINA GEORGE!

If you weren't writing contemporary romance, what genre would you write?

Probably thrillers, because I love the concept of this fast-paced, edgy story that keeps you guessing. The problem with writing romance novels is that it's addicting. So while I've had great story ideas for thrillers, I never really do anything with them because romance is always my go-to. And anyone who knows me knows I'm a romantic at heart!

Of all of your characters, which ones seem the most real to you and why?

I would have to say Kate and Mac from my original Publicist series seem the most real. The reason is hard to explain, but I think at her core Kate is a lot like me, or who I'd like to be all the time. She's flawed but confident, she makes bad choices and owns up to them. I can 100% relate to that.

In terms of Mac…well, that's a bit of interesting backstory because I dated a "Mac" that the character was modeled after. It wasn't as perfect as this contemporary romance character, of course. But he's where I got the idea. No, we didn't stay together, which in the end was for the best. But in romance novels you've got to have a HEA (happily ever after).

You're being held hostage by the last show you watched, who is holding you captive?

Great question! I'm being held hostage by the folks in Grey's Anatomy, which is sort of fitting for this interview since the show often cycles around the relationships that live and die within the walls of that hospital.

Also, I'm still not over Shonda Rhimes killing off Derek.

If you had to pick, where would you rather write? Noisy coffee shop or a quiet library, and why?

Coffee shop, without question. I love the noise element of it, which is odd—but I guess great for the creative juices. Also, there's always coffee at the ready. And snacks, a romance author has to have her snacks!

You're having a dinner party and can only invite five people—living or dead, who would they be?

Tom Petty for sure, and probably Prince so they could jam out. Princess Diana, without question. I'd invite ABBA (can they count as one person?), former President Eisenhower, and Amelia Earhart. Cool group, no?

Do you have any writing superstitions? Or funky/odd writing habits that you want to share with our readers?

I don't know about superstitions per se (though I'm not opposed to smudging my office after a particularly bad afternoon of writing), but I do create a book playlist on Spotify that I can listen to, while I'm writing. If I'm struggling with a particular character, I'll find a song for them and play it on repeat. I do that a lot, with a song on repeat, too. And not just a character song but a song that gets me into the vibe of writing contemporary romance.

What's a song that you hate people talking over?

Without question: Follow You, Follow Me by Genesis—it's from the 1970s and I simply adore it.

I had her post this under the Editorial Reviews section in the back end of Author Central and, voilá, more places to use keyword strings! It's a great, fun little tool to not only add some interesting content to your Amazon book page, but also use those keyword strings again and again!

10 SMART WAYS TO LAUNCH YOUR BOOK ON AMAZON

Creating an outstanding book launch is something every author aspires to do. However, for most of us the problem is that there's always so much going on around the time you launch your book. Maybe you're planning a book launch party, some local signings, or even a big virtual event. There are a few key elements specifically related to your Amazon launch that shouldn't be overlooked. There's an organic algorithm that also kicks in if a book launch is done correctly. The algorithm, once it kicks in, can sustain a book for a long period of time, and getting it to kick in, is a combination of a few things we'll discuss in this chapter.

For many authors, having that "new release" banner is ideal, but having the word "bestseller" attached to it is even better. Your book can sit, successfully, on the new release bestseller list, but there are a lot that factors involved in order for this to happen.

Genre, for example, makes a difference in how long your book sits in the new release category. The number of books launching at the same time (on the same day) as yours is also a factor. The third factor is algorithm, which is something you absolutely can control, and is easily woven into your book launch. The following steps don't require a huge effort, just a bit of planning ahead. If done right, they can pay big dividends in terms of the Amazon boost all new release titles get.

PRE-ORDER

We discussed pre-orders earlier, but allow me to reiterate some points here.

I don't recommend this for all authors. If it's your first book, and you have no real platform, I'd skip it. Why? Because a pre-order is a great tool if you're ready to hit the ground running when your book launches.

If you do a pre-order and launch your book, but it takes a month or months to get reviews, it can actually hurt your exposure on Amazon. The system is geared to pushing books that are selling right out of the gate. If you decide to do a pre-order, don't do a long one. Two weeks or a month at the most, and be prepared to move quickly when your launch date arrives.

FREE BOOK TEASER

While this isn't a new release strategy, it is a great tool for boosting your overall book exposure. Here's how it works: Put the first few chapters of your book up as a free book edition. Meaning it's a **permafree** book sample with a link to your complete book. I've done it for mine, but the idea originally came from a David Baldacci title, which had a seven-chapter free preview to help boost the launch of his latest book. Here it is below:

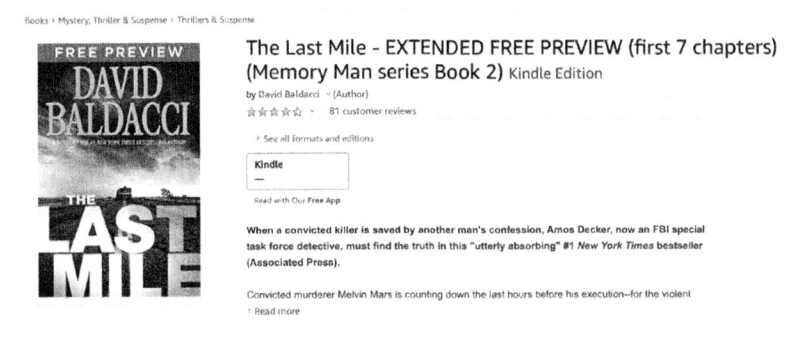

Books › Mystery, Thriller & Suspense › Thrillers & Suspense

The Last Mile - EXTENDED FREE PREVIEW (first 7 chapters) (Memory Man series Book 2) Kindle Edition

by David Baldacci (Author)

★★★★★ ▾ 81 customer reviews

▸ See all formats and editions

Kindle

Read with Our Free App

When a convicted killer is saved by another man's confession, Amos Decker, now an FBI special task force detective, must find the truth in this "utterly absorbing" #1 *New York Times* bestseller (Associated Press).

Convicted murderer Melvin Mars is counting down the last hours before his execution—for the violent

‹ Read more

This isn't the first time Baldacci has done this, and frankly it's brilliant and quite easy to do!

BOOK DESCRIPTION

Make sure your book description is sharp, focused, and impactful. Don't cram your entire description into one unreadable paragraph. Make sure your description has lots of white space, because remember: we scan, we don't read. And attention spans have shrunk from 20 minutes to an astonishing 8 seconds.

Remember, you don't have a lot of time to get readers interested in your book. Lead with a strong headline, and don't bury your most important point at the bottom of the book description, because a reader won't get that far. This is something to keep in mind for your existing titles as well as for any new book launches.

SOCIAL PROOF

If your book is up for pre-order, it's a great goal to figure out fun ways to urge readers to post reviews quickly. By quickly, I mean within the first week after the book goes live.

Sometimes authors complain that reviews get pulled when they go live too fast (meaning within 24 hours of the book launch), but I haven't seen that as a consistent problem.

I've had books that have gone live and almost immediately started earning reviews. Rarely have they been pulled, but I know it does happen to a few authors, so proceed with caution, because nothing can kill a book launch like having reviews appear and then disappear on Amazon!

BOOK AND EBOOK PRICING

Another element of a successful book launch is your pricing, and I recommend getting a bit creative with this. Generally, I like to start a new book launch off with a slight price discount for the eBook or print book (though it's often easier to do this with the print book). Starting a book off at $2 below what the standard pricing will be is a good way to boost early exposure. If you discount your eBook in particular, you could also boost it with eBook promos, which I'll address later.

AMAZON KEYWORD STRINGS & CATEGORIES

While this may seem counterintuitive, I'm going to suggest that you hold off doing keyword strings and categories right when the book launches on Amazon. Why? Because you gain a certain amount of momentum for a book while it's in the 'new release' arena. This can last for up to a month, as I mentioned previously.

What I'd suggest doing is adding keyword strings that include the term "new release romance" (or whatever your genre is) and then removing those after three weeks and adding in your final keyword strings, as well as adjusting your categories. I know a lot of authors who do this right at the launch, but I like holding off on that strategy until the momentum from the new release begins to diminish. The second batch of keyword strings helps give the book another boost after the initial momentum starts to fade.

AMAZON ADS

I'd recommend starting Amazon ads prior to book launch if you're doing a pre-order. I suggest running them two weeks prior to your book launch date.

ALSO-BOUGHT

It's often tempting to send an email blast out to your family and friends to encourage them to buy your book. This is a strategy you should use cautiously, because often it will skew your Also-Bought results if readers (who don't normally buy in your genre) click on your book. I've covered this in great detail in a previous chapter, just remember it can hurt, not help, your book launch algorithm—save inviting everyone you know for 60-90 days down the road.

BOOK LAUNCH, EBOOK PROMOS

I love doing eBook promos, and it's especially fun to do them while your book isn't at full price (yet), and you can still take advantage of the book launch sale you've got going. Plan to do at least one of these at the three-week mark of your book launch. This helps to keep the new release spike going too!

SPREADING OUT YOUR BOOK EDITIONS

One of the final options to extend the new release buzz is to separate out your release of editions of your book. For example, you may decide to release your eBook first, with your paperback, hardcover and audio following at later intervals. Each new edition of your book is a new book release, spacing them out can help you gain new momentum each time a new edition launches on Amazon.

DISCOUNTED EBOOK PROMOTIONS

Promoting your discounted eBook is great way to boost your exposure on Amazon and help spark the algorithm. Know, however, that not all price promotions are equally effective. It's more important to be strategic than to be fast. I used to always talk about free eBook promotions, but I'm now finding that discounted eBooks do equally well—so long as the discount is substantial.

TIMING YOUR EBOOK PROMOTION

Ideally you should wait until your book has been up on the Amazon site for a while before you offer a price discount. I've found that waiting ninety days is best. If you're doing a price discount only, you can do that virtually any time, but for freebies, you'll want to give your book's sales figure a chance to grow on its own.

PRICING AND REVIEW STRATEGIES

In addition to timing, pricing and reviews are two aspects of eBook promotion that can make or break sales.

Generally, I don't recommend starting any type of campaign like this (whether paid or free) without having *at least* eight to ten reviews on your page. With the many discount specials offered nowadays, most consumers won't go for a free or heavily discounted eBook with a naked Amazon page (a page with no reviews).

Right after the eBook campaign you'll continue to see a lot of traffic on your page—the residual momentum you've created from the promotion. I've seen it last up to three days. If your book did well during the promotion period, this momentum will help it rise higher in your category, since the promotion helped trigger the internal Amazon algorithm.

If your promotion was a freebie, keep in mind that your book will pop onto a different list, it goes over to the "free eBooks" side of Amazon.

Which means that it could hit bestseller status on that list, although since it's free, the term "bestseller" is more a nod to ranking, not book sales per se.

For free eBook promotions, remember that the right post-freebie pricing when it returns to the paid category will also help perpetuate this algorithm. If the book did well, it might be tempting to list it at a higher price. However, I recommend that you keep your pricing low during the days immediately following your free promotion. How low? It depends on how your book was priced in the first place, but generally I suggest you discount it by half for just three days.

This may seem counterintuitive. I mean, you want to make money, right? What better way to sell tons of books at full price by capturing the tsunami of traffic finding its way to your page because of your freebie?

You do want to make sales, but don't think short-term. Think long-term. If you can boost your book within a category with the right pricing, it will help to trigger a sales momentum you would never get otherwise. By keeping your book on your readers' radar screen by having it show up higher in the category, you'll have more long term sales.

EBOOK PROMOTION

Even if everyone loves a good sale, you can't just put the book up on Amazon, mark it free, and call it a day. You have to promote it.

There are a lot of sites that let you list your book for free (see below). During your promotion, you should also be on sites like Twitter, sending messages, using hashtags, and pinging other accounts.

Here are websites and Twitter accounts I know would love to hear about your freebie, followed by a list of hashtag suggestions. Make sure you plan your freebie at least two weeks in advance, because sometimes listings on sites require that much notice. There are some paid listings, too. I've had good success with BookBub.com, Kindle National Daily, and Book Gorilla.

Here's a List of Free Sites Where You Can List Your Book

https://katetilton.com/ultimate-list-sites-promote-free-ebook
www.ereadernewstoday.com

www.pixelofink.com
www.indiesunlimited.com/freebie-friday
www.kindlenationdaily.com
www.totallyfreestuff.com
www.icravefreebies.com/contact
www.kboards.com/free-book-promo
www.indiebookoftheday.com/authors/free-on-kindle-listing
www.kindlebookpromos.luckycinda.com/?page_id=283
www.thedigitalinkspot.blogspot.com.es/p/contact-us.html
www.freekindlefiction.blogspot.co.uk/p/tell-us-about-free-books.html
http://freeebooksdaily.net
www.freebookshub.com/authors
www.frugal-freebies.com
www.ereaderiq.com/about
www.askdavid.com/free-book-promotion
www.ebookshabit.com/about-us
www.snickslist.com/books/place-ad
www.awesomegang.com/submit-your-book
www.goodkindles.net/p/why-should-i-submit-my-book-here.html
www.kornerkonnection.com/index.html?fb=ebookkornerkafe
www.dailycheapreads.com
https://bookgoodies.com/authors-start-here
www.indiebookoftheday.com

TWITTER ACCOUNTS TO NOTIFY

@DigitalBkToday
@kindleebooks
@Kindlestuff
@KindlebookKing
@KindleFreeBook
@Freebookdude
@free
@free_kindle
@FreeReadFeed

@4FreeKindleBook
@FreeKindleStuff
@KindleUpdates
@Kindleebooks
@Kindlestuff
@Kindlemysbook
@Kindle_Freebies
@100freebooks
@kindletop100
@kindleowners
@IndAuthorSucess
@FreeEbooksDaily
@AwesometasticBk
@Bookyrnextread
@Kindle_promo
@KindleDaily
@Bookbub

HASHTAGS TO USE

#free
#freekindle
#freebook
#kindlepromo
#freeebook

Discounted eBook promotions are a great way to boost your overall exposure on Amazon, plus they can earn more reviews to help populate the page. I love doing freebies and discounts—I've often seen big sales bursts after a campaign has ended. One of the main reasons for this burst is because of the residual traffic still going to your book page after the promo has ended.

You can also promote your book with special pricing. Kindle Countdown Deals offers an opportunity to promote special pricing across a few days.

You pick the pricing, and you pick the days. Many of the free sites mentioned above will also let you promote your book if it's $0.99, which is another great way to get your book out there. Be aware, though, that the idea behind Kindle Countdown is to literally count down via your pricing. If you start the deal at $0.99, it goes up to $1.99 the next day, and so on until it's back at its regular price. We've found that too many different price points confuse the consumer. Pick one price, do Kindle Countdown, and just let it run for three to five days.

SUPPORTING YOUR PROMOTION WITH ADS

I always encourage authors to consider many different ways to support their own work. Don't make one book promotion strategy fend for itself. If you're planning a promotion, in addition to promoting it on sites that will list your book, or getting other accounts to Tweet about it, you should consider supporting it with ads.

While Amazon ads and social media ads have their place, the platforms are pretty complex. If you already know how to run those kinds of ads, definitely do it. But for those of you who are new to ads, or aren't comfortable enough with them yet, I have a solution: BookBub ads.

BookBub ads, unlike BookBub promotions, are available to all authors without restrictions, so you can bet you're already a sure thing.

HOW TO COMBAT THE DISAPPEARANCE OF AMAZON REVIEWS

Disappearing reviews on Amazon are a pretty consistent problem for most authors, in fact some of my older blogs posts addressing this issue are some of our most popular posts, overall. This tells me that despite Amazon pulling back on being so aggressive with their review pulls, many authors still wrestle with this. If this is an issue you've faced, these tips may help you deal with it. Keep in mind that if this is impacting your book regularly, there may be a broader issue with the book, and I'll address that as well.

PRESERVE WHAT YOU'VE ALREADY GOT

Here's the scenario…you've got a dozen new reviews and suddenly half of them are missing. What do you do?

My suggestion is to keep a close eye on new reviews as they pop up and there's an easy way to do this (especially if you have multiple books). Just access the "Customer Reviews" on the backend of your Author Central page on Amazon. That tab will show you all your reviews, across all of your books. You can easily screengrab this page regularly and note when reviews are missing.

How does this help you? Well, when reviews get pulled, you still have the actual review, which you can then repost to the "reviews" tab under each specific book under Author Central.

Yes, you'll still lose the review on Amazon, but you've at least preserved it to add to your book page. I do this regularly: once a week if I'm in between book releases, and more frequently if I'm on top of a new book release.

SOMETIMES AMAZON HAS A GLITCH

Though Amazon would never admit this outright, their website isn't perfect. Glitches happen all the time. It's understandable with a site that enormous.

The same is true for book reviews. In fact, just last week I had three separate people tell me that their review got pulled (they had emailed me to ask why this would happen). The interesting piece was that it was for different types of books, and the only unifying factor was that the reviews were all posted around the same time. I emailed each of them and told them to try and repost the review. Two of them did, and the reviews have gone live.

Bottom line, if some of your reviews are pulled (and you have the screen capture mentioned above to verify this), you might want to write to Amazon to see what's going on, or call them via the Help button in Author Central.

I find that if you're reasonable, polite and patient, Amazon Author Central will gladly help you. I've contacted them for all sorts of issues and have gotten assistance.

One thing I will say is, don't be emotional. I know it's hard when your book is losing reviews, so you may want to give it a day or two before you tee up a help email. But if you can do so professionally, engaging in a conversation with Amazon could be really helpful.

In some cases, you may find it was a random glitch—I've actually known authors to inquire about missing reviews on Amazon, and then get them all back. It's worth a shot if you feel like the reviews you lost were from credible sources i.e. legitimate book buyers/readers.

KEEP PUSHING FOR REVIEWS

Okay, maybe this sounds obvious, but a lot of times what happens is authors (at some point) stop pushing their readers for reviews. You can't replace reviews you've lost—and even if you are one of the lucky ones and have never lost a single review, you'd like to keep adding to the number of reviews on Amazon, yes?

There are a couple of quick ways to do this.

The first is the Dear Reader letter in the back of the book. This letter thanks the reader for reading and invites them to review your book on Amazon.

The second is to just ask for reviews. If you have a mailing list, and even if you don't, asking for reader reviews is something authors rarely do. Those who do ask, reap the benefits.

If you don't have a mailing list, consider putting out the request on social media, but do so in a way that makes your reader feel like they're truly helping you. Remind them how helpful reviews are to the buying process, how their voice matters—how their input (good or bad) could help to persuade a buy. Remember, never ask for five-star reviews, just an honest assessment of your book.

The issue of disappearing reviews is a tough and ongoing one, and often it doesn't seem like a fair fight. I've seen products on Amazon with a crazy number of extremely similar reviews—in one case all the reviews had the exact same wording and were all left up on the product page. But sadly, it's part of doing business on Amazon, which is why I suggest the simple but powerful tips in this piece to keep policing your reviews, keep getting new ones, and take your issues to Amazon when you feel there's been an error.

TURNING YOUR BOOK INTO A 24/7 SALES TOOL

Let your book go to work for you. You can use the book itself to encourage reviews.

One of our clients, a first-time, unknown author, was ready to market her book. We knew that, given her genre—contemporary romance—the potential for receiving reviews was low. We decided to encourage reviews by having her write a request letter to her readers to include at the end of her book. In her letter, she politely asked for feedback and a review. She now has nearly 70 reviews on Amazon. Simple, but effective!

And remember, she was a first-time author with no online history—and she self-published. Even with all these things working against her, she got tons of reviews. Were they all five-star? No, but let's face it, a book page populated with tons of five-star reviews is often considered suspect anyway. All her reviews were authentic, written by real readers the author became engaged with. What's more, those readers are now part of her "tribe." She stays in touch with them and lets them know whenever another one of her books comes out.

For her second book, we encouraged her to actually write a letter explaining how tough it can be to get reviews and encouraging her readers to review her book(s) on Amazon and Goodreads. She also thanked them for buying her book.

The result was amazing. Here's the letter, if you'd like to try it out for yourself. Do note that the style of the letter should be revised for whether you're a fiction or nonfiction author. Feel free to copy this or revise it—whatever you feel works for you—but use it. It works!

Thank you for reading!

Dear Reader,

I hope you enjoyed *Shelf Life: The Publicist*, book 2. I have to tell you, I really love the characters Mac and Kate. Many readers wrote me asking, "What's next for Nick?" Well, be sure to stay tuned, because the saga of publishing drama isn't quite over. Nick will be back in book 3. Will he find his happy ending? I sure hope so.

When I wrote *The Publicist* book 1, I got many letters from fans thanking me for the book. Some had opinions about Mac and Kate, while others rooted for Nick. As an author, I love feedback. Candidly, you're the reason I will explore Nick's future. So tell me what you liked, what you loved, even what you hated. I'd love to hear from you. You can write me at authorchristinageorge@gmail.com and visit me on the web at www.thepublicistnovel.com.

Finally, I need to ask a favor. If you're so inclined, I'd love it if you would post a review of *Shelf Life*. Loved it, hated it—I'd just like to hear your feedback. Reviews can be tough to come by these days, and you, the reader, have the power to make or break a book. If you have the time, here's a link to my author page, along with all my books on Amazon: http://amzn.to/19p3dNx

Thank you so much for reading *Shelf Life*, and for spending time with me.

In gratitude,
Christina George

Just a few things about this letter.

First, you can't ask for just good reviews.

Second, a lot of people may read this as an eBook, so be sure to put a live link in the book, preferably a link to your Amazon Author Central page. When you're putting your book together, you won't have the actual link to the Amazon page it's on. Of course, you want your readers to see all your books, not just the one they're reading.

Be sure to add this letter to the last page of your book, not the front matter. A lot of authors like to write letters to their readers, but that's not the purpose here. You want to thank them for reading a book they just finished. If your request is at the front, they'll forget about it by the time they get to the end.

THE BENEFITS OF CROSS-PROMOTION

Another way to engage readers is to attract them from one book to the next. Generally, when you are reading a book on Kindle and you get to the end of the book, it will send you over to the book's page and ask you to rate it. One thing the Kindle device doesn't do is send readers to the actual author page on Amazon, where they can find out about the author's other books. Kindle's in the business of selling books, so referring you to the Also-Bought section makes more sense for them, but the same's not true for you. Crosspromoting your books is an invaluable sales strategy.

OTHER WAYS YOU CAN CROSS-PROMOTE YOUR BOOKS

- List your other titles with excerpts at the back of your book. If you have too many, pick two or three, and vary which ones you mention in each of your books, meaning that in book X you reference titles A and B, and in book Y you mention books C and D, and so on.

- Create a special offer that links to your website or, ideally, takes them to a special page on your website directing the reader to your special offer. Maybe as a thank-you give them a free download of one of your books or novellas, or if you've written non-fiction, a workbook, a quiz, a checklist, etc. In exchange for this freebie, you get their e-mail address. This does two things: First, the freebie builds goodwill with your reader, and second, you're collecting their e-mail for future promotions.

> **BONUS TIP:**
>
> Get a URL that best describes your niche. For me, it's www.SellMorebooksonAmazon.com. This URL has (in the past) forwarded to my Amazon author page. Now it goes to our Master Amazon Video Program.

HOW TO RESPOND TO A REVIEW

Most of the time when we get reviews, they're good. Sometimes they're even great. Occasionally, though, you may get a review that's not so great.

Unfortunately, not everyone will love your book. When that happens, just let it go. But before you do, thank the reviewer for reading your book anyway. They may ask you if you still want them to run the review. The choice is yours, of course, but unless it's truly bad and meant to be hurtful, every review deserves at least a response.

HOW TO RESPOND TO REVIEWS USING AUTHOR CENTRAL

When you log onto your Author Central account, look for the blue bar at the top. You'll see a button for customer reviews.

amazon Author Central   Author Page   Books   Sales Info ∨   **Customer Reviews**

This button will take you to the page shown below, where you'll see a bunch of your reviews. Under each review you'll see the, "Add a comment," button, where you can respond to reviews. It's a great way to connect with your readers on Amazon!

Here's a screenshot:

1. **New! Kindle Customer** reviewed The Publicist Book One and Two
   ★★★★ 4.5 September 24, 2020
   The characters are so realistic at moments up love them then you hate them, You pick put what you don't like bout them and find the qualities you really relate to. this is a roller coaster ride that is realistic, it reminds you life
   View on Amazon.com   Add a comment   View this book's reviews on Amazon.com

2. **New! Nate D** reviewed Climax: The Publicist, Book Three
   ★★★★★ **Kate's story** September 21, 2020
   This was Kate's story. An intriguing read. I received a free copy of the book. And am voluntarily leaving my honest opinion.
   View on Amazon.com   Add a comment   View this book's reviews on Amazon.com

3. **New! Mandi** reviewed Climax: The Publicist, Book Three
   ★★★★★ **great** September 21, 2020
   I am voluntarily reviewing this book after receiving a free copy. Loved this book and the characters. Definitely hard to put down!
   View on Amazon.com   Add a comment   View this book's reviews on Amazon.com

REVIEW INCENTIVES

If you have a gift that ties into your product—swag—it's totally fine to send it to the reviewer. Seriously. Reviewers *love* swag, as long as it's classy and not junk.

Incentives can be a great way to pull in reviewers, so send swag with your book. We offered a book-themed tote bag for the first 25 reviews on one book and ended up getting almost all 25 reviews overnight because fans were so eager to get the tote bag.

Be creative. There are lots of charming, fun, and often useful things, such as a tote bag, which can promote a book's location or theme or represent a protagonist's personality. You can also find useful things that are often associated with your topic. A couple more examples include a novel set in Belgium that was accompanied by a small box of Belgian chocolates, and a motivational title sent with practical pocket journals.

Just make sure you tell your reviewers you want an honest review, good or bad.

Keep it on the up-and-up—unlike the guy who was so desperate to get reviews he offered an all-expenses-paid cruise for the best review but had no intention of actually providing the cruise. While this wasn't illegal, it was unethical. The author got a lot of reviews, but he also had several people post reviews on his Amazon page calling out his scam. Not a smart approach in the end.

One of the best incentives you can offer your reviewers is to express sincere gratitude. Always, always, always send a thank-you, either with the book or after.

Even if you don't like the review, thank them anyway. You'll cast your net even wider if you do.

Reviewers talk. Be grateful, no matter what. They'll genuinely appreciate that.

GIFTING EBOOKS

Gifting eBooks is fun way to use the Amazon.com system. You can gift eBooks to reviewers who request a MOBI (Kindle-formatted) copy of the book, or you can gift them to various readers to help generate buzz and drive sales.

Be sure to drop the price of the book before gifting, though, because the gifting process will cost you less if you do. I generally drop the price of my book to $0.99 before gifting. And while it'd be nice to gift your book during your freebie giveaway time, Amazon won't let you. The book has to be at a certain price point—whatever pricing you determine.

Gifting a book does not necessarily mean everyone will actually download it, because they can use the price of the book to buy something else. I keep the pricing low so that it's too much work to flip it into something else and much more appealing to download your book.

When you gift the book, Amazon will send you to a form you can fill out with any message you want to include. Just complete the form and hit "Send."

You will be charged per book you send, but you will *not* be paid royalties until the recipient downloads it. That means if they don't see the e-mail notification—if it winds up in spam or whatever—you'll still be charged but won't get your cut. You can circumvent this problem by sending the book to people you actually know. That way they'll be more inclined to download it. Be sure to send them an e-mail in advance to let them know it's coming, so if it doesn't show up in their inbox, they can check spam.

Gifting eBooks can help spike sales statistics, especially if everyone is downloading the book on the same day.

As a final tip, if you want to spike your book in a particular category, encourage your friends or followers to download immediately so it'll have a greater impact on your Amazon presence!

BONUS RESOURCES

Here are some free downloads to help you get focused, get organized, and start selling more books!

Monthly Book Marketing Planner: Start filling this out to ensure you have a strategic book promotion strategy laid out in advance, saving you the stress of coming up with ideas on the fly, or missing crucial book marketing opportunities altogether.
www.AMarketingExpert.com/monthly-book-marketing-planner

Quarterly Amazon Planner: Feel confident that you're keeping up with all your Amazon updates and optimization strategies throughout the year.
www.AMarketingExpert.com/quarterly-amazon-planner

Blog Outreach Tracker: Use this to keep track of your ongoing blogger pitching, requests, and more!
www.AMarketingExpert.com/blog-outreach-tracker

Reader Profile Brainstorm: Save time, money and a lot of guesswork, and avoid missed opportunities by creating a fresh reader profile that will really help you zero in on where you need to be focusing your efforts, and on the best sales angles to use for your buyer markets.
www.AMarketingExpert.com/reader-profile-brainstorm

GET MORE READERS!

Remind people they don't need a Kindle to access eBooks. Whenever you do a book promo, mention that readers can access your book through all of these resources:
- Kindle Cloud Reader: https://read.amazon.com/about

- iPhone and iPad apps: www.amazon.com/gp/feature.html/ref=k-cp_iph_ln_ar?docId=1000301301

- Android app: www.amazon.com/gp/feature.html/ref=kcp_and_ln_ar?docId=165849822

- BlackBerry app: www.amazon.com/gp/feature.html/ref=klm_lnd_inst?docId=1000468551

SPECIAL OFFER

ARE YOU SELLING ENOUGH BOOKS ON AMAZON.COM?

If you're ready to take your Amazon sales to the next level, consider our Master Amazon Video program, which is a companion to this book. The video series is designed to walk you through everything, step-by-step.

Get unlimited access to the membership platform, with new videos being added all the time!

FIND OUT MORE AT
www.AMarketingExpert.com/master-amazon-video-series.

**And be sure to use the code below to get
$100 off of our $199 program!**

PROMO CODE:
truckloadvideos

ABOUT PENNY C. SANSEVIERI & AUTHOR MARKETING EXPERTS, INC.

Penny C. Sansevieri, Founder and CEO of Author Marketing Experts, Inc., is a bestselling author and internationally recognized book marketing and media relations expert. She is an Adjunct Professor teaching Self-Publishing for NYU. She was named one of the top influencers of 2019 by New York Metropolitan Magazine.

Her company is one of the leaders in the publishing industry and has developed some of the most innovative Amazon Optimization programs, as well as Social Media/Internet book marketing campaigns. She is the author of 18 books, including "How to Sell Your Books by the Truckload on Amazon," "Revise and Re-Release Your Book," "5-Minute Book Marketing," and "Red Hot Internet Publicity," which has been called the "leading guide to everything Internet."

AME has had dozens of books on top bestseller lists, including those of *The New York Times*, *USA Today*, and *Wall Street Journal*.

To learn more about Penny's books or her promotional services, you can visit her web site at www.amarketingexpert.com.

Printed in Great Britain
by Amazon